BFI FILM CLASSICS

· ·

Rob White

SERIES EDITOR

Edward Buscombe, Colin MacCabe and David Meeker

SERIES CONSULTANTS

Cinema is a fragile medium. Many of the great films now exist, if at all, in damaged or incomplete prints. Concerned about the deterioration in the physical state of our film heritage, the National Film and Television Archive, part of the British Film Institute's Collections Department, has compiled a list of 360 key works in the history of the cinema. The long-term goal of the Archive is to build a collection of perfect showprints of these films, which will then be screened regularly at the National Film Theatre in London in a year-round repertory.

BFI Film Classics is a series of books intended to introduce, interpret and honour these 360 films. Critics, scholars, novelists and those distinguished in the arts have been invited to write on a film of their choice, drawn from the Archive's list. The numerous illustrations have been made specially from the Archive's own prints.

With new titles published each year, the BFI Film Classics series is a unique, authoritative and highly readable guide to the masterpieces of world cinema.

The best movie publishing idea of the decade.
Philip French, *The Observer*

A remarkable series which does all kinds of varied and divergent things.
Michael Wood, *Sight and Sound*

Exquisitely dimensioned ... magnificently concentrated examples of freeform critical poetry.
Uncut

Agnes Moorehead as Aunt Fanny

BFI FILM CLASSICS

THE MAGNIFICENT AMBERSONS

·············

V. F. Perkins

bfi Publishing

First published in 1999 by the
BRITISH FILM INSTITUTE
21 Stephen Street, London W1P 2LN

The British Film Institute
promotes greater understanding and
appreciation of, and access to, film and
moving image culture in the UK.

British Library Cataloguing-in-Publication Data
A catalogue record for this book is available from the British Library

ISBN 0–85170–373–9

Series design by
Andrew Barron & Collis Clements Associates

Typeset in Fournier and Franklin Gothic by
D R Bungay Associates, Burghfield, Berks.

Printed in Great Britain by The Cromwell Press, Trowbridge, Wiltshire

CONTENTS

. . . .

For Toby Perkins and Polly Perkins, with love

The mansion under wraps: George Amberson Minafer with Aunt Fanny

1

. . . .

PRODUCTION AND DESTRUCTION

A study of *The Magnificent Ambersons* will keep speaking of it as a ruin and treating it as one of the great tragedies of movie history. I recognise that, in the state to which its owners reduced it, the picture careers between brilliance and banality, its very worst scenes being the ones that RKO Pictures imposed to wrap the story's finish in rose-tinted cellophane. But my main concern will be with Orson Welles' film as one of cinema's glories – an incisive, moving, generous and thrillingly accomplished work. I shall not spend too long on the studio's part in first enabling and then wrecking the production.

An efficient outfit would not have made the film at all. After the first unhappy previews in March 1942, the company president George Schaefer wrote a gutless letter to Welles complaining that there had been particular trouble with the Pomona audience that had gone to the Fox Theatre to see *The Fleet's In*: 'In Pomona we played to the younger element ... who contribute the biggest part of the revenue. If you cannot satisfy that group, you just cannot bail yourself out with a $1,000,000 investment.'[1]

Schaefer should have seen it coming. Welles delivered what we must suppose he had promised, a remarkably close adaptation of Booth Tarkington's 1918 Pulitzer prized novel. All the problems that the film encountered were predictable if anyone at RKO had taken the trouble to read *The Magnificent Ambersons*. Tarkington interwove a family saga with social history at the turn of the century so as to portray the rise of a mid-western American city – Indianapolis in all but name. His 'study of a triumphant family becoming submerged' was a hazardous subject for a movie. It required the reconstruction of an extravagant way of life that would first be displayed and then traced through the transformations caused by the rise of the automobile. The setting alone made it a difficult and inevitably an expensive project.

Early estimates on Welles's *Ambersons* script put the production cost at close to one million dollars. Welles undertook to cut back. But the final figure that Schaefer presented for his board's approval, agreed in September 1941, was above $850,000. The decision was remarkable. RKO Pictures was once more in a state of near-bustitude, having emerged from receivership as recently as January 1940. Now like other Hollywood companies it was suffering the effects of the war in Europe in the reduction of its foreign earnings. But it was less able to withstand that loss because of its films' poor performances at the US box office. A crisis in mid-1941 had necessitated borrowings to keep the studio in operation. One of the conditions of a three million dollar loan had been an undertaking to set $750,000 as the upper limit for all production.[2]

At the top of the studio's scale you would expect to find starry properties packed with commercially promising ingredients and supplied, above all, with a clear and gripping emotional line. Tarkington's novel tells a story of failure and frustration; its key events are deaths, and disappointments passively endured. His text carries a warning against dramatisation; a young audience in the theatre would, he says, be 'not only scornfully amused but vaguely angered'[3] by his tale of middle-aged romance between the prospering car manufacturer Eugene Morgan and the widowed Isabel Minafer (née Amberson), heiress to a declining fortune.

While that is the novel's most appealing relationship the main thread of the narrative is carried by Isabel's only child, George, the product of her loveless marriage to the pallidly respectable Wilbur Minafer. Adored and indulged by his mother George grows up in idleness with an arrogant conviction of superiority that makes the townsfolk long for his 'come-upance' [sic]. As a young man, George falls for Eugene's daughter Lucy. But when his father's death frees Isabel to respond to Eugene's love, George is outraged. On a pretext supplied by Aunt Fanny Minafer's report of a gossiping slight on Isabel's reputation, he turns Eugene from the house, and breaks with Lucy to take his mother abroad, away from Eugene and from the imagined interest of the townsfolk. Thwarted in this late hope of romantic fulfilment, Isabel wastes away. She dies essentially of a broken heart.

There are two unavoidable issues. Why is Isabel's union with Eugene so vile a prospect for her son? Why can Isabel, threatened with heart-break, not bring herself to face George down and insist on her own right to happiness? Answering these questions in ways that adequately motivate the key events required the clear and forceful presentation of the bond between a young man and his mother in its least attractive and potentially most embarrassing aspects. The actions and motives are not hard to credit. The threat was that audiences might not be willing to understand, and might retreat from discomfort into impatience or contempt.

In addition a time span of about twenty-five years presented difficulties in casting, performance and make-up to compound the awkwardness of a bumpy construction whose stops and starts might break, or kill, dramatic momentum. It may have been reasonable to rely on Welles' genius to solve those problems. But the ending of Tarkington's novel was another matter, a desperate patch-up that had to bring Isabel's voice across from the Spirit World in order to promote a reconciliation between Eugene and a George ennobled by adversity. Tarkington had contrived the semblance of a happy ending, for a story whose logic would not go that way. Injured by an automobile in a street accident, the pauper George received hospital visits first from a radiant Lucy with 'ineffable eyes', then – following ghostly guidance – from her father. We were left with the assurance that the romance was on again, and that that was a good thing. Finally Isabel's love was allowed an unearthly consummation, and her death was to some degree undone, by having Eugene realise that in forgiving George he 'had been true at last to his true love, and that through him she had brought her boy under shelter again. Her eyes would look wistful no more.'

It seems extraordinary that any studio head would schedule a major production without having satisfied himself that solutions had been found for this Tarkington Problem. Since fidelity was, at the end, impossible the adaptation would need to invent a finale that would be actable and powerful, plausible but not flatly depressing. The earlier, silent, version of Tarkington's tale that Vitaphone released in 1925 as *Pampered Youth* had evidently found its answer in a radical departure from the novel's events as well as from its title.

In 1939 Welles had done a radio digest of *The Magnificent Ambersons* with his Mercury Theatre on the Air for a broadcast in the Campbell Playhouse series. He had both narrated and taken, with intermittent conviction, the role of George. At the end Eugene (Walter Huston) had soliloquised a letter to the dead Isabel. That device allowed the play to present, but avoided the need for it to enact, the events of Tarkington's conclusion – minus, of course, the séance. A clever device for radio, but no good for the cinema.

George Schaefer listened to a recording of the broadcast and agreed on *The Magnificent Ambersons* as the property for Welles' second film. He fell asleep during the playback, or so Welles claimed. The claim is plausible because nothing indicates that Schaefer raised the questions about the finale that the broadcast would surely have provoked, even in an executive with so marked a lack of movie sense. It seems that Welles was without a resolution for the Tarkington Problem when in the fall of 1941 the production was okayed. The shooting script carried a version of the radio ending but there is evidence that Welles was unconvinced by it. The storyboards drawn by Joe St. Amon[4] to visualise the first draft screenplay are extensive and detailed but they run out at the point where George is a stretcher case about to be taken to hospital. Since the storyboards were an important element in the preparation of the physical production their absence suggests that Welles was not yet ready to commit himself to an ending.

He had spent July–August 1941 writing the screenplay, having borrowed King Vidor's yacht for the purpose. He had performed a remarkable cut-and-paste job on Tarkington's text, drawing on the novelist's spectacular gifts for dialogue with flavour and monologue with character and colour. No doubt the work was propelled by ideas on casting. There can never have been any question – it must have been one of the attractions of the material – that the plum roles of Eugene Morgan and Aunt Fanny Minafer would go to Joseph Cotten and Agnes Moorehead, members of the Mercury group who had come to Hollywood with Welles. Another of the gang, Ray Collins, would be perfect for George's Uncle Frank on-screen as in the broadcast.

Since Welles was not seeking a powerful star from outside his group for any of the main roles – for Isabel, say, or Lucy Morgan or George – the project escaped one of the more gruelling disciplines of Hollywood production where scripts were routinely reassessed and reworked to make the leading roles attractive to suitable actors with box-office pull. The part of George went to Tim Holt, a contract player at RKO whose B-Westerns were a regular source of profit. From an artistic viewpoint Holt was an inspired choice, and perhaps Schaefer was pleased to see the casting budget held down here, as in the hiring of newcomer Anne Baxter for Lucy and of Dolores Costello, a star of the silents persuaded out of retirement to play Isabel.

But there were two further results. On a risky project RKO was going well beyond its budgetary ceiling with no slice of the expenditure allocated to the star salaries that might secure a basic element of box-office appeal. A specific consequence was that there would be no injection of star charisma to offset the objectionable aspects of the leading character and that George Minafer would be likely to stand at the film's centre as an unvarnished figure of youthful self-obsession: maladroit, self-righteous, humourless and insensitive – like many of us at that (or any) age, but not what we expect of a movie hero nor of the object of the leading ladies' affections.

In his scrutiny of the *Ambersons* project Schaefer may have been distracted by relief at seeing Welles engaged with a subject that threatened neither contemporary relevance nor political embarrassment. In April 1941, with turmoil obstructing the release of *Citizen Kane*, he had turned down Welles' script for a Mexican-set thriller (*The Way to Santiago*) whose villains were local fascists in league with the Nazis. Turn of the century Indiana would have looked much more comfortable, and the novel offered the kind of prestige investment that Schaefer favoured, often to the studio's cost.[5]

Shooting started on 28 October 1941, after five weeks in which Welles rehearsed his cast. A month later an assembly was made of three scenes. One of them was that of the great winter ball in the Amberson mansion, a section that would display the film's virtuosity in presenting the lavishness of the Amberson mode of life. Alongside this, representing the bleaker and more strident aspect of the film, were two later scenes: one in which George embarrasses the family by discourtesy to Eugene during after-supper conversation ('Automobiles are a useless nuisance...'); the other the subsequent encounter on the great staircase between George and his aunt in which Fanny lets slip strategically that a romance between Isabel and Eugene is causing gossip round the town, and then goes into panic at the force of George's reaction.

The show reels were screened for Schaefer and the man whom he had made the baffling decision to appoint as production chief on the west coast, Joseph Breen (until recently the Hollywood censor). On 3 December (four days before the bombing of Pearl Harbour took the USA into the Second World War) Schaefer cabled Welles with his response:

> Your current picture ... is chock full of heart-throbs, heartaches and human interest. From a technical standpoint it is startling ... I

am very happy and proud of our association. Congratulations and best wishes.

Completely absent was any cautionary note about expense. The scenes reviewed would have given clear indication of the factors that were going to result in overruns on the schedule and the budget: the intricate and necessarily laborious approach that made the camerawork startling, and the extended construction of the sets – most fully displayed in the ball scene – that accommodated the choreography of action and viewpoint. The cable is from a man so delighted with the results that he has no room for pettifogging quibbles over cost. That is a fine attitude for a film-maker, but ominously inappropriate in a studio chief.

Principal photography was completed towards the end of January 1942. At some point, during rehearsal or while shooting, Welles hit on an amazing solution to the Tarkington Problem. He would have Eugene pay a visit to Fanny in her mean little rooming house to tell her what has happened at the hospital and how he feels. The 'happy ending' news of reconciliation between George and Lucy, and Eugene's conviction of final truth to his true love, would be bracketed within a culminating instance of Eugene's insensitivity to Fanny and Fanny's consequent inability to share in his wistful sense of fulfilment. As filmed, Agnes Moorehead's participation in the exchange was so minimal that the scene became virtually a monologue for Eugene punctuated and punctured with dissonant elements – the creaking of Fanny's rocking chair and the distant playing on a phonograph record of a comic vaudeville patter.

We shall never see this. We can read the dialogue and a shot-by-shot description in the continuity script that Robert L. Carringer has edited as The Magnificent Ambersons *A Reconstruction*.[6] And in one of the few really indispensable books on the movies – *This is Orson Welles*, edited by Jonathan Rosenbaum[7] – we have Welles' remarks to evoke the mood:

> If only you'd seen how [Agnes Moorehead] wrapped up the whole story at the end.… Jo Cotten goes to see her after all those years in a cheap boarding house and there's just nothing left between them at all. Everything is over – her feelings and her world and his world; everything is buried under the parking lots and the cars.… And there were all these awful old people roosting in this sort of half old

folks' home, half boarding house. They're playing cards in the background, and others are listening to that record, with the elevated clanking by.... That's what it was all about – the deterioration of personality, the way people diminish with age, and particularly with impecunious old age. The end of the communication between people, as well as the end of an era.... I wish the film at least existed.

That the film does not exist is due to a chain of circumstances some of which seem likely to remain obscure. We know that Welles rushed to conclusion his work on this movie and his many other commitments in order to undertake a goodwill filming mission to Brazil at the request of Schaefer and of the US government. He worked on a rough cut with his editor, Robert Wise, and he recorded his commentary for the soundtrack, during a stopover at the Fleischer studios in Miami in early February 1942. Wise and Jack Moss, business manager for the Mercury Theatre, were left with full authority to see to all the detail in post-production fine tuning ready for an Easter opening, but Welles expected to be able to vet the result and make the last refinements when Wise would bring the completed movie to Rio for his approval. For whatever reason, that never happened. Material from the cutting rooms was sent to Welles for comment which he wired or telephoned from Rio but the opportunity to make a final cut with Wise was never granted. The first sign of trouble came with a cable from Wise on 16 March:[8]

> Dear Orson: ... Mr Schaefer unexpectedly requested running *Ambersons* today for himself and Koerner and four other men unknown to me probably Eastern executives. Following showing Schaefer enquired regarding shortening length. He has ordered me to prepare picture for sneak preview Tuesday Nite with following cuts: both porch scenes and factory....

It is noteworthy that Schaefer was already talking about studio changes before the first preview. Then, faced with hostile reactions in Pomona, he promptly sought legal advice on the studio's entitlement to make its own version of the picture. After a second preview in Pasadena on 19 March Schaefer wrote the previously quoted letter,[9] sent to Welles in Rio by special delivery. His account of the reactions:

Never in all my experience in the industry have I taken so much punishment or suffered as I did at the Pomona preview. In my twenty-eight years in the business, I have never been present in a theatre where the audience acted in such a manner. They laughed at the wrong places, talked at the picture, kidded it, and did everything that you can possibly imagine....

Schaefer was repeatedly scathing about the sombre quality of Bernard Herrmann's score – as if sombre were self-evidently an inappropriate mood. In remarking that 'cutting will help considerably' he made it clear that his report was designed to provide a rationale for imposing radical changes. Unfortunately, Schaefer and his fellow executives were not alone in their panic reaction to the previews. Welles' Mercury colleagues were recruited into the view that drastic action was needed to make the movie palatable. The Easter release was abandoned, and Wise was put in full charge of the editing, which meant that he was authorised to decide for himself how much notice to take of the instructions and appeals received from Welles in Brazil. Since the studio was going to make changes, and those changes would certainly include slashing down the 131 minutes of the first cut in an attempt to put some zip into its designedly steady pacing, Welles' colleagues tried to keep the initiative so as to save what could be saved of the quality of the work as they saw it. But that made them collaborators in the destruction. The figure who behaved with most integrity and artistic discretion was the irascible Bernard Herrmann, never one to protect his career at the cost of his musical judgment. He refused involvement and threatened RKO with the law if they displayed his name as composer of a score no longer wholly his.

The movie that eventually emerged corresponded in many respects to a scheme drawn up by Robert Wise and Jack Moss with the involvement of Joseph Cotten; it was communicated to Welles in a lengthy wire despatched by Moss three days after the second preview.[10] (Welles responded that he could not see the remotest sense in their suggestions.) Early in April Schaefer issued the instruction for retakes (which involved rewriting by various inexpert hands) and appointed Wise to construct a 'releasable' picture. Material was shot or re-shot under the direction variously of Wise, Moss and the assistant director Freddie Fleck. The film was cut and cut again in the light of further previews in early and mid-May. Schaefer commanded some final excisions and restorations before calling a halt (8 June) and approving a print for release.

We see the film in the version that he authorised, eighty-eight minutes long. Since that includes material that Welles did not direct, and could not have directed, the loss is of more than fifty minutes. In the picture's first half we are deprived mainly of scenes and sections discarded to bring down the running time. One can imagine that Welles himself might have arrived at a few of these cuts. But in the second, bleaker, part the cutting, re-ordering and alteration amount to a travesty. The chopping and changing in the scenes of George's opposition to his mother's romance show the studio in a ridiculous fix, working to dilute the impact of the drama's outstanding feature. Preview reactions have been allowed to determine what goes out, what comes in, and what goes where without apparent concern for dramatic shape and thematic coherence.

Worst of all is the ending. It is an amazing instance of what can happen in film-making by committee. It attempts to go back to Tarkington's happy-sad finale but uses the remnants of Welles' design. If you are going to do Tarkington's ending you might as well get up the courage to stage the reconciliation scene in the hospital bedroom. You cannot do the Tarkington mood and attempt to compromise with Welles' version by retaining his involvement of Aunt Fanny, especially as played by Agnes Moorehead. Her Fanny Minafer is a distillation of the pain and bitterness that the pretty world ignores. It makes no sense to bring her on at the end, coated in syrup, to rejoice in George's redemption and Eugene Morgan's dream of fulfilment.

The RKO finale: Eugene and Fanny

The Mercury team moved away from the ambitions declared in the wake of the first previews: 'to remove slow spots and bring out heart qualities of (the) picture.'[11] Under Schaefer's command they reworked it into a different film. If it had to be shortened, there was a lot of merit in the single hefty cut volunteered by Welles. This would have eliminated all the material dealing with George and Isabel's absence in Europe so that her illness and death would result immediately from George's rebuff to Eugene and the strain of the conflict between love for her son and love for Eugene. That cut would have made one big change to the plot and it would have binned a couple of wonderful scenes that survive in the RKO version. Welles told Peter Bogdanovich that in suggesting such a cut he was 'bargaining. "I'll give you that if you'll leave me this."'[12]

Evidently he was trying to protect the overall design of the film – the movement from the remembered hope of springtime into a world of regret and decay – and, as the climax of that movement, the end with Fanny in the boarding house. But he could do nothing to protect the film from improvement because its fate was bound up with the fate of the studio boss. George Schaefer's managerial record was, more and more clearly, disastrous. In every month since August 1941 the RKO production arm had lost money. Too many of his prestige investments had flopped. He had not built the balanced programme that sustained the successful studios where bread-and-butter movies took care of the overhead while, among the bigger projects, risks that failed were covered by risks that paid off.

As a result his position had become the subject of factional struggles among the stockholders. Wise's reference to Charles Koerner and the four Eastern executives who attended Schaefer's viewing may be one indication that *The Magnificent Ambersons*, as the studio's big release for Easter 1942, was being drawn into the power plays within the corporation. (Koerner had replaced Joseph Breen as production head in March, by order of the RKO board; a Koerner regime was to replace Schaefer's – with swift success – when the latter was ousted in June 1942.) Welles was the most prominent of Schaefer's protégés, in part because the most productive, and his position was a matter around which many a skirmish was being staged.

These may be the reasons why Schaefer was unwilling to do what other moguls had done when faced with expensive movies that turned out to have dubious box-office appeal: accept the gamble in a robust spirit and try to give the picture effective support as it went to the theatres to meet its fate. Schaefer had invested in Welles as an innovator, yet now he complained that the boy wonder had not supplied a commercial, by implication conventional, product. The post-preview letter to Welles bleated at its close 'Orson Welles has got to do something commercial. We have got to get away from "arty" pictures and get back to earth. Educating the public is expensive....'[13]

Once the studio head decided (or agreed) to take the timid way out, tacking and trimming in response to preview reactions, *The Magnificent Ambersons* was doomed. (There had been no previews on *Citizen Kane*.) By the time of its release, Schaefer was no longer in charge at RKO. In Welles' regularly repeated view *The Magnificent Ambersons* was purposely released so as to fail because '[the] takeover in RKO brought in new bosses committed, by the simple logic of their position, to enmity.'[14] Evidence in support of his claim might be found in the decision to put the picture out unsuitably doubled with the Lupe Velez programmer *Mexican Spitfire Sees a Ghost*. However *The Magnificent Ambersons* does not seem to have been completely abandoned, since it was nominated for four oscars, including best picture of the year.

We can sympathise with Welles' wish to believe that, given the chance to supervise the cutting, he would have been able to save the picture,[15] or that its release could have been managed so as to produce success. But I am willing to suppose that it could not have been an audience pleaser in the wartime circumstances of 1942 or perhaps in any circumstances yet encountered. (Equally, I do not doubt that it would have been less of a disaster – declared loss $624,000 – in part because its cost would not have been inflated by the outlay on RKO's changes.)

I can accept that Welles may simply have lacked the popular touch. That might give a studio reason not to employ him as a film-maker. But it provides no justification for first employing him and then, when he has delivered the movie you commissioned and made you a masterpiece, destroying it rather than attempting to find it whatever audience might be available. There is testimony from witnesses who saw the Welles' *Ambersons*. Anybody who speaks for her or himself about the film, rather than about the experience of the previews, speaks of it with reverence. Apart from Welles himself, who was consistent in claiming that it was far superior to *Citizen Kane*, we have reports from the composer Bernard

Herrmann, cutter Mark Robson and director Cy Endfield who attended a studio showing.[16]

Robert Wise sought to excuse the job done on the film by conceding that as a work of art, it was 'a better picture in its original-length version: as an *accomplishment*. But we were faced with the reality of not art, but business, and what to do with something that wouldn't play.'[17] It is a sad fact, commercially and in its consequences for some major artists, that a number of the greatest movies do not 'play'. *The Rules of the Game* (Renoir, 1939), *Madame de ...* (Ophuls, 1953) and *Vertigo* (Hitchcock, 1958) are among the examples because for many people they do not work on first viewing. You have to know the shape of the whole picture, even of its surprises, before you can become involved in its process. The Renoir and Ophuls films share another aspect with *The Magnificent Ambersons*. In each of them you need to free yourself from the standard expectation that the characters are there to be liked or admired; but you can find, if you allow yourself to dislike them, that you come to love them.

It is my belief that there has been a discipline, and one on balance healthy for the art of movies, in the commercial pressure to make films that can be enjoyed at first contact and without special preparation. Yet the casualties of this healthy discipline have been impressive. Who can tell whether a movie that withheld its pleasures and insights from a first viewing has any to offer to a second? One of the merits of a director-centred approach to cinema is that it can prompt us, in the face of a picture by a gifted film-maker that seems boring, baffling or botched, to ask whether the fault may be not in the movie so much as in our way of looking at it. Whatever its immediate pleasures or problems, the work of the great directors should challenge us as the pianist Artur Schnabel was challenged by 'music better than it can be played'. The thrills and rewards of criticism come from trying to rise to achievements we know to be larger than our understanding.

2

. . . .

MAGNIFICENCE – DEW-BRIGHT MORNING

We start with the word, the spoken word. In the darkness after the removal of the brief, bald opening title we hear words that claim authority. They declare knowledge of the origins of things: 'The magnificence of the Ambersons began in 1873.' And knowledge of their destiny: 'Their splendour lasted throughout all the years that saw their Midland town spread and darken into a city.' The sentences glory in achievement through the reiteration of 'magnificence ... splendour' and by giving more stress to duration (in 'lasted') than to transience. For all that, melancholy haunts these buoyant phrases. Magnificence is already over as the account begins and its end is linked to growth, the loss of a town and a loss of light. We are being told that our business is with time and change, with the connection between things that grow and things that fade and fall under shadow. Though the word is withheld, we are being told here as in the title that our concern is to be with family.

Beginning with the spoken word, we begin with the voice. A black screen gives additional weight to the voice when, after a pause, it sounds out of the darkness. The speech is deliberately paced, reflecting the confidence of one who knows that he has no need to excite us with a rush of information. By the end of the first phrase we recognise the voice. Its enchantments were already familiar in 1942. One of the famous sounds of a century that produced a new relationship between celebrity and the voice, Orson Welles' speech has a beauty, character and presence to rank with the song of Bessie Smith, Tauber, Bjorling or Sinatra.

Welles had been quicker than anyone to appreciate, and more successful in applying, the lessons in microphone technique offered by the popular entertainers, the clowns and the singers – pre-eminently by Bing Crosby. The comics and the crooners taught new ways to use the voice now that the microphone had freed it from the demands of projection. The solo voice could dominate without strain, carried in softness to the back of the balcony; if stress were heard, it was heard as the stress of emotion. The gap narrowed between the actor's use of voice and the character's manner of speech. (The gap is at its widest – a different thrill – when the diva socks out the dying thoughts of the opera heroine.) Welles' mastery of the microphone was the product of intuition honed by experiment and practice in the radio work that was the basis of his stardom. Close-miked speech gave authority to tones of fireside intimacy.

The depth of Welles' rich bass-baritone wants the jargon *phonogenic*, since the microphone so admires the relaxed, expansive quality that sounds out the fullness of the chest rather than the tightness of the throat. The pitch of the voice allows an emphatically masculine authority to provide the matrix for delicacy and sentiment. It is an astonishing thought that this is the voice of a man in his twenties since a vital part of what it constructs is an air of maturity and experience. It has the sound of one who has lived a lot, seen a lot, and already found quite a deal to regret.

For an actor with Welles' remarkable breath control, relief from the demands of the auditorium created new possibilities in phrasing that allowed the line of a speech to be tightened or stretched or interrupted – Billie Holiday style – with great rhetorical flexibility. Listen to the way Welles charms and teases with the pacing of the first line. He suspends the word 'magnificence' by a slight separation of its first syllable and by equalising the remaining three. Then a tiny beat prepares a graceful fall onto the next phrase. A shorter beat after 'Ambersons' and the tone becomes more inward; that their magnificence began in 1873 is not a piece of historical data that needs to be impressed on our memories. This is not a lecture but a confidence, so the history of these Ambersons is for reminiscence and unlikely to demand a place in the annals. A weakened emphasis on the date means that we absorb not the year but the notion of pastness – of a point within the stretch of living memory – and we pick up the sense that although origins are significant our concern will not be with them.

In a pause just after the opening statement, music enters – a distant music matching the voice in softness but setting off its depth with the strains of a high violin, starting solo and soon accompanied by floridly tumbling figures on a harp. This is the first presentation of 'Toujours ou jamais', the 1878 waltz by Emil Waldteufel (1837–1915) that will offer the themes for much of the score. It is a music of lost loves and fading hope, where all that can be kept is the sweet pain of recalling what was always, but only, about to be. As the parlour music of a bygone time, the waltz introduces nostalgia both as a mood and as a subject. It is distanced from the vernacular music of 1942 America but more remarkably from the governing conventions of Hollywood film composition. The distance is first proclaimed in a silence: by omitting to support the presentation of the title with a mood-setting overture to ease us into the film, the music has refused the pervasiveness that signifies a background role. It begins only when the voice has completed its first period, and it comes in at a pause so that it neither competes nor merges with the spoken words. Rather it enters into duet, and the duetting relationship is accomplished before a third element is introduced with the delayed fade-in of the image.

Anachronism is deployed in both the instrumentation and the performance. Grandeur of orchestration in the symphonic mould of Korngold and Steiner is renounced and the single voices of violin and harp replace the massed forces of the studio band. The violin is played with the willed sweetness and smoothness of an outmoded virtuosity that smiles through tears but throbs with emotion so as to let us know the bravery of its smile. The harp meanwhile ripples through a different mode of display; its busy fingerwork offsets the fiddler's yearning legato with a show of concentration and accomplishment.

Still in darkness we listen as Welles continues. The mood is unhurried enough to hold off even the presentation of a picture – conventionally, the beginning of the movie – and the gentle delivery of the words helps to evoke an era without noise and without rush: 'Their splendour lasted throughout all the years that saw their Midland town spread and darken into a city.' Welles shapes the long line in a way that directs attention to its poetry as well as to its data. As his quiet conveys a raptness of engagement with old times, the pitch and rhythm of the speech enact its sentiment; he extends the vowel of 'spread' to put the sense of reach into the ring of the word, and he steps down onto 'darken' and 'city' to offer a sound-image of decline.

His speech turns the meaning of the opening words. The voice does not match itself to 'magnificence' and 'splendour'. Those words ask for assertive delivery to boost their claims on the public eye and ear. They are passed over by tones that respond to a personal mood of fondness and regret. We are told that the Ambersons had magnificence, but what we hear is that they have the speaker's heart. It is possible that his attachment is to their frailty more than to their pomp.

The accompanying music reinforces the sentiment in the narrator's voice; it ignores the text's assertion of glory and picks up on the speaker's tone of nostalgia. But it goes further. By presenting the music of the late nineteenth century in the perspective of the mid-twentieth, it evokes structures of feeling that characterise the era of antimacassars and parlour recitals. While it shows that this sentimentality has not entirely lost its appeal in the passage through the jazz age it also displays the artifice of its rhetoric and thereby colours the way we hear the speaker.

In putting the reading of Tarkington's text ahead of its dramatisation *The Magnificent Ambersons* became one, perhaps the first, in a vital line of movies that seek artistic integrity in the manner of their fidelity to their literary sources. Welles' narration, like the film's dialogue, is closely derived from Tarkington's text. The commentary in the opening section arranges fragments from the novel's first fifty pages and digests them into a new continuity but it adds almost nothing to the author's inventions. As a result Welles 1942 speaks in the prose of Tarkington 1918. The plump rhetoric has a period ring in an era when the prevailing American literary mode had been set by so clipped and airless an opening as 'The door of Henry's lunchroom opened and two men came in.'[18] Tarkington's literary mannerisms put a further mark of distance between us and the about to be depicted past.

Through words and music that announce it as a period piece the film calls into question the viewpoints and attitudes that it will seek to dramatise, offering its own sentiments as tokens of a lost way of life for which regret is only one of the available responses. A regime of irony offsets the novel's view of American history, its exclusive validation of the perspective of the prosperous white middle class. So it is that the voice of Orson Welles, the first director's voice to be known as such by the American movie audience, can work as both evidently the voice of the author and yet not unquestionably the voice of the film.

Now that we are so used to voice-over, and can even hear it as observing formulas characteristic of one kind of 'old movie', the originality of Welles' approach is no longer obvious and certainly not shocking. We need to remember that in 1942 Welles was working for an audience most of which had grown up, as he had, with the silents. In terms of influence on Welles the vital precedent seems to be Sacha Guitry's extraordinary movie *Le Roman d'un tricheur* (1936) where the soundtrack is all but monopolised by the hero's recollections, though Thornton Wilder's narrated play *Our Town* (1938) can not have been far from his mind. In American cinema, though, the off-screen voice was common only in newsreels and, most relevantly, in documentaries like Pare Lorentz's *The Plow that Broke the Plains* (1936) where the explaining function of the lantern-slide lecturer had been developed to work poetically as one element in a sound montage with music and effects. The reporter's voice assumed an authority – speaking fact or speaking consensus – that could become hectoring in the volume, speed and insistence of its delivery.

In fiction movies the narrating voice was rare; it was always that of a participant in the action, most often the central character, who would be seen as well as heard and nearly always seen before heard. It was the voice of reminiscence. It could prepare us for a move back in time, as at the opening of *Rebecca* (1940) with the woman's words 'Last night I dreamt I went to Manderley again…'. This voice represented the consciousness that was reflected in the structure of images and the selection of events. Its use cued subjectivity, and the possibility of error.

The blank screen at the opening of *Ambersons* displays the absence of the speaker and points up the fresh path that Welles negotiates between the modes of the documentary and of narrated fiction by bringing together the authority of the unseen newsteller and the subjectivity of a participant. The voice and manner participate in emotion, but the words are detached from the action: '*their* splendour … *their* town'. This narrator is not telling us about his own life and memories and he will never come into the film as an 'I'.

And now the image.

Its fade-in follows a shift in the narration. From summarising an era ('… all the years …') it moves to detailing moments in a daily routine. Welles allows the sentences to lengthen and he incorporates more of Tarkington's florid indirectness and strategic repetition:

In that town, in those days, all the women who wore silk or velvet knew all the other women who wore silk or velvet and everybody knew everybody else's family horse and carriage. The only public conveyance was the streetcar. A lady could whistle to it from an upstairs window, and the car would halt at once, and wait for her, while she shut the window, … put on her hat and coat, … went downstairs, … found an umbrella, … told the 'girl' what to have for dinner … and came forth from the house.

There is match and mismatch between what we hear and what we see. The commentary specifies a social class and some actions, like finding an umbrella, but no personalities: 'A lady could whistle …'. is more distant and general than 'When Elvira Hardy whistled …'. This generalising aspect of the commentary is echoed by the remoteness of the picture. The foreground is empty and in the middle distance – too far off for individual features to register – costumed figures enter the image in patterns that bear out some of the speaker's claims. The screen is crossed by groups of women dressed and hatted with uniform respectability (that is to say with an ordinary rather than an extravagant extravagance) and a pair of carriages whose occupants wave an exchange of greetings. Then comes a well-filled horse-drawn conveyance that bears the legend 'Western Midland Transit Co. No.1' and that stops on a woman's request.

The town is represented by the road and sidewalk with their sparse traffic and by the single dwelling beyond, sufficiently held off from any neighbouring property to stand alone in the picture. Not a mansion, not a setting for magnificence, but a large house dressed in gothic whose architecture declares a concern for both privacy and community while it testifies also to the solid but unflaunted prosperity of its owners. The lady who opens the upstairs window to hail the tramcar would have to be a member of the 'silk or velvet' class. The camera's viewpoint is governed by the decision to frame this one house whole, as the stable background to the movements of persons and seasons, yet the building that determines the structure of the image has no similar place in the spoken account.

The authority of the narration is enhanced because it stays in command of the soundtrack. We see a lot of noisy activity, yet – with one momentary exception – we hear nothing of it; its sound is suppressed in favour of Welles' voice while Herrmann's music continues in its vein of pathos, making no response to the liveliness on show. Also, the knowledge of what is out of sight is elaborated in the speaker's account of action within the house and, even more, in his accommodating pace. His pauses seem to observe the woman indoors and to grant her the time to complete each item of her business; the emphatic synchronism between commentary and image seems to be continued, although it is suspended, in this tally of unseen doings. The device evokes – by appearing to draw on – the reliability of routine. If the speaker can respond to what is going on inside the house, that is not only because he occupies a storyteller's place of knowledge but partly as well because those events are what

Yoohoo!

The opening shot; action
distant and unmentioned

would of course be happening, on this occasion as on so many others.

The stability of routine reflects an imperceptible gradualness in the rate of change. A world is being proposed in which tomorrows would be like yesterdays in comfortable succession. That is the unspoken ground on which, in the movement and pacing of this opening shot, the film's thematic concern with time and with pastness is fused with the way it shapes its own time. The opening statement reaches completion in a remark that deviates from Tarkington to stress the gap between the world we are seeing and the one from which we – both the audience and the narrator – are looking: 'Too slow for us nowadays, because the faster we're carried the less time we have to spare.'

As with Willa Cather, as with Max Ophuls, the past is offered as the past because it is rendered inaccessible even as it is reconstructed. While the mood is one of empathy with *those days* rather than with *nowadays*, there is distance and tension between the narration and the image. This is brought about by agitating the friction between the generality of the spoken account and the particularity of the image.

The report of the lady's actions is verbatim from the novel; but while the words dwell on what was regular and predictable, and is largely invisible, the activity displayed on-screen is specific and different: the passengers bustle down from the streetcar and busy themselves to heave it back onto its track while the driver tries to calm a fractious horse. The commentary offers a presumption of elegant ease that much of the action upsets. The one sound that reaches us from the on-screen world is the woman's cry of *Yoohoo!* from her upstairs window. It pierces the narration to anticipate – and challenge – the reference to her 'whistle'. The woman's shout across open terrain violates the intimacy of the storytelling, and the violation is stressed through an acoustic clash. Her shrill call is recorded distantly but mixed at a level to chop into the smooth flow of Welles' deep, soft, closely recorded speech. This is the first strong indication that the world is not going simply to fall in with the speaker's view of it.

The conflict is furthered at the climax of this section by the woman's coming forth from the house at a run, in haste to catch the streetcar. This occurs at the point where word and image seem to be converging again as the described action off-screen emerges into visibility. Yet the woman is hurrying aboard, decorum not her first concern, as Welles begins his remark on her world as 'Too slow for us nowadays…'. The perspective is beautifully judged to register how what counted as hurrying in that world can look leisurely from the one that has replaced it.

In the development cued by the first of Herrmann's variations on the Waldteufel tune Welles maintained the framing as he carried the image through a series of transformations, through winter to summer, from day to night, while his narration expanded the claim that

> In those days they had time for everything: Time for sleigh rides, and balls, and assemblies, and cotillions, and open house on New Years, and all-day picnics in the woods, and even that prettiest of all vanished customs, the serenade. Of a summer night, young men would bring an orchestra under a pretty girl's window, and flute,

harp, fiddle, cello, cornet and bass viol would presently release
their melodies to the dulcet stars.

Tarkington's rhetoric has reached a climactic ripeness with 'dulcet stars'
but here the second assertion of on-screen sound brings an abrupt clash
with Herrmann's gentle strains and with the narrator's pretty
generalities. The talk of courtship and music gives way to the sight and
the noise of splintering breakage as a young serenader teeters backwards
to smash down onto his instrument, the bass viol whose melody the
speaker had promised.

At the same time the quality of the image is violently changed. In
key respects the climax of this sequence reverses the terms of its opening.
We start with an image evoking both theatre and early silent cinema, with
the proscenium-framed general view of the action seen distantly and seen
whole from an immobile point at the centre of the front stalls. Movement
is across the screen in straight lines matching the horizontal plane that is
particularly marked by the white woodwork of the house and of the
tramcar. The one movement in depth stays in agreement with the boxed-
in view; the woman's emergence from the house requires no adjustment
of viewpoint or focus and it works like an entrance through the door at
upstage centre. Jerkiness at the fade-in and vignetting round the borders
of the image offer more evocations of pastness through their reminders
of early cinema and old photographs. Lap dissolves effect the progress
through the hours and seasons cinematically, but the succession of fixed
frames is like a process of lantern slides while the on-screen lighting
changes replicate the stage magic of a transformation scene.

In moments, everything is overturned. The stateliness of the
distant view and the fixity of the proscenium collapse in a disorderly swirl
when the frame tilts down to hold onto the toppling figure revealed to us,
once head has rolled under heels, as Joseph Cotten. His tumble into the
foreground breaks the frame and transforms the space of the image.
Perspectives abruptly shift from theatre to cinema as the focus is pulled to
fix the sprawled body in close view while his fellows lurk beyond at
matchstick scale. With figures close and distant picked out by the
lighting, composition in depth replaces the lateral emphasis. The
modelling effects both of the wide-angle lens and of the low camera
position now come into play. For the first time a figure is personalised by
the camera's interest in his thoughts, his feelings, and the results of his

27

Composition in depth: Eugene
floored

actions. We look into his eyes to see where they are looking, and their concerned gaze further expands the space by opening up a non-theatrical world, the one on the other side of the camera. Cotten (whom we shall discover to be Eugene Morgan) stares up and out submitting to the judgment, or appealing to the indulgence, of an observer off-screen and above – one whose viewpoint is sharply distinguished from ours.

All at once the vacancy of the foreground, which had been unremarkable as an aspect of the proscenium view, is transformed. The camera's vision is now set *within* the world which it had observed before from a zone removed and without character. The transformation of space is matched to a changed sense of time. Rapidity, suddenness and surprise mark the image now; this frame shares and displays movement where the earlier one had absorbed it. For the second time the flow of music and narration is punctuated by 'real' sound of a challenging character. The crash is timed to put an ironic exclamation point after 'release their melodies to the dulcet stars'. In its aftermath nothing is spoken, but the music slows and weakens to mark the event, with regret, as a crisis. The newly opened space of the scene is extended now as the young man's look of appeal is answered by a young woman's reproving glare.

The introduction of Isabel Amberson at the moment of her rift with Eugene Morgan completed the film's first section in narrative terms. In visual terms the completion involved a further move from theatre to cinema; the change from a fixed to a mobile camera was followed here by the first cut – to a close-up of Dolores Costello looking out from a lace-curtained window and not smiling. Her undressed hair suggests that the racket of the failed serenade has drawn her from her bed. She is seen from outside and below. These elements of Eugene's viewpoint colour the image so that the close view seems – even while it cannot embody Eugene's physical eyeline – to register his concern for her reaction, and his awareness of her displeasure as she turns away. With no cut back to Eugene the climactic image of this introduction is/was of Isabel's disappointment and her withdrawal.

All this is in the film as we have it, but the design is weakened by re-editing. The first presentation of the town (in the shot with the tramcar) is separated from the 'Time for everything …' series that ends in the serenade débâcle. Breaking the flow constructed by Welles, RKO brought forward the montage on male fashions that should have functioned as preparation for Eugene's attempt at making up with Isabel. The object was presumably to conventionalise the narrative by completing the introduction of place and period – the establishing material – before starting the significant action. Welles had worked differently, to overcome the distinction between character, plot and setting by having the characters of the story appear first as incidents in the picture of the town. The studio's changes disrupt the development both of Herrmann's pattern of theme and variations and, more intrusively, of Welles' narration so that 'In those days they had time for everything…' no longer enters easily onto the ground prepared by 'Too slow for us nowadays…'. Worse, Tarkington's cherishable simile – 'Against so homespun a background the magnificence of the Ambersons was as conspicuous as a brass band at a funeral' – has been deprived of its foundation since it now follows a section, anything but homespun, on style and show rather than coming after the reflections on thrift deleted from Welles' version.

The Magnificent Ambersons still begins effectively, but the changes to Welles' opening are hard to forgive. The released version shed very few frames but its rearrangement of the material unpicked a perfectly designed and, on all the evidence, perfectly executed seed image for the entire film. 'Image' needs to be understood in a large sense here; in terms of film form it is like a musical phrase offering a first statement out of which the main developments will be generated. The figure was one that took us in ninety seconds from a bright, stable, horizontally composed view of a leisurely, harmonious community to a disordered, night-bathed but dynamic image in depth of collapse and disappointment. The drama shows trivial circumstances – the stuff of slapstick – that determine a

Isabel at the window

course of incomprehension and bitterness for the next generation. Within a nostalgic evocation we are brought to our first sight of Isabel and Eugene, and it sets a pattern. Isabel is a Rapunzel whose prince arrived drunk, and stumbled when he should have climbed. We see her frustrated within the house. Eugene is outside and floored.

These visual relationships are to have great importance in the progress of the drama – not only Eugene's exclusion from the house but also the witnessing of it from indoors and upstairs. With Isabel dressed only in hair and lace, and seen with the censor-baiting closeness that licenses the mind by confining the eye, the window that screens her must be her bedroom's. When she lets the lace curtains fall back across her face as she turns away, it is as if she has re-clothed herself. But while the image plays up the sexual aspect of the hopes here foiled, it does so ambiguously. The representation of Isabel troubles erotic promise with suggestions of the maternal. In the first place, while she is offered as one of those 'pretty girls' who used to be serenaded, and while our view of her is brief and veiled, the glimpse is of a mature rather than a girlish presence – no large effort having gone into transforming the face of an actress in her mid-thirties. With Isabel looking down from indoors on the mischief outside, Welles fixes the maternal cast to her image and primes us for the confusion in her role between the lover and the mother. He prepares her to become the subject and object of courtships that cannot be avowedly sexual, and that assume their own defeat.

It was Welles' invention to bring together in contradiction the commentary on the vanished charms of the summer serenade and the depiction of Eugene's misadventure. Tarkington had these in passages ten pages apart and very distinct in tone; he completed the catalogue of modes and manners before he began the introduction of individual characters. The collision and blending of different elements and contrasted textures, most of them derived from Tarkington, enabled Welles to surpass the novel even while maintaining fidelity to it.

The rhythmic effects of simultaneity and succession, doubling and contradiction that are available when sound punctuates speech, or when the screened events first enact and then negate the claims of the narrator, constructed a rich fabric in which irony and enchantment interwove; a world was densely realised at the same time as it was called into question. The staccato effects of the 'Yoohoo!' and the breakage were interruptions in a play with continuity that kept the image within a fixed structure while the incidentals of light and dressing changed with the hours, seasons and traffic. Welles made one 'long take' out of four shots, and then set that way of treating time and space, with its emphasis on fixity and flow, against the turbulence of the mobile frame and the discontinuity of cutting.

Alongside this a different composition of the sustained and the momentary emerged from the treatment of the soundtrack. The suppression of natural sound, in relation to figures distant but active and visibly communicating, gave them a spectral air. Real sound intruded twice into the flow of the narration and the music. In each case the sound was isolated from its acoustic context; we did not, for instance, hear the sliding of the sash as the lady closed her upstairs window. The intrusions came, though, in a different pattern and a different cadence: the lady's 'Yoohoo!' was heard in sync with a small (because far off) displacement in the image; after it, the commentary resumed, in a rhythm that measured its repetitive stretch, to itemise her unremarkable doings. By contrast the crash came after the completion of Welles' comments on the serenade and in contradiction to them. It accompanied an event closely viewed to fill the screen with movement. In the second case, unlike the first, the upheaval in the image was in scale with the explosion of noise. But now the commentary held its pause and the sequence ended with the narrator speechless over the first event and the first actors to have drawn the camera's intimate attention.

In Welles' version this was the place for the sequence which surveys changing fashions in menswear, and so resumes the engagement with the community's modes and mores. The commentary's disavowal of the recent mishap would have been blatant because it carries on, as if nothing has happened, in the cataloguing manner with which it was just now presenting transport issues:

> During the earlier years of this period while bangs and bustles were having their way with women, there were seen men of all ages to whom a hat meant only that rigid, tall silk thing known to impudence as a 'stove-pipe'. But the long contagion of the 'Derby' had arrived: one season the crown of this hat would be a bucket, next it would be a spoon....

As before, this narration is geared to changes in the image. Nothing of moment escapes its notice or outruns its knowledge. But the delivery is now brisker, and without the marked pauses that before seemed to testify that it was keeping track of – and dependent on – the way the world presented itself to the camera. Now the images are being displayed on a different time-scale, one set by a commentary whose language and manner have become overtly humorous, encouraging amusement at the quaintness of times gone by. The third of Herrmann's variations on 'Toujours ou jamais' scampers beneath as various sections of the orchestra chatter their disrespect back and forth over the mock solemnity of a recurrent oom-pah.

The changed relationship between the world and its depiction is marked formally through a new deployment of continuity and fragmentation. A seminal aspect of the opening statement was its play between the duration and stability of the image, and the extremes of selectivity applied to the soundtrack. But in the fashions sequence real sound is completely suppressed so that narration and music flow without interruption while the techniques of montage are transferred to the image.

The introduction of an approach based on the discontinuity of isolated visual moments is strongly signalled in the first three shots. Of course, their concern has not shifted from that town, those days and that class, and they have a specific connection through the common factor of prominent top hats. Otherwise a careful disparity brings into succession a changing number of different characters seen from contrasted angles and distances in different actions in different locations at different times of day and in different seasons – all within the space of fifteen seconds.

The major loses his hat

The boating lake

Even the degree of abstraction differs. A saloon bar and a boating lake are the manifest locations of the first two shots. The third shows an old man whose stove-pipe hat gets hit by a snowball; he is seen in close-up and from below, against a background white enough to support the sense of a snowy outdoors but so flat and blank as to set him in a featureless space.

In these shots we are seeing the figures who will become Wilbur Minafer and the old Major Amberson, and we may identify the woman with a parasol out boating with an attentive young man at the oars: the same (Isabel Minafer to be) as the object of the failed serenade. More reliable is our recognition of the viol-smasher in the next section. The hat series carries over into a fourth shot that takes us indoors to re-introduce Joseph Cotten as he tries the effects of two differently crowned bowlers. A trick image seems to share his viewpoint looking into an oval mirror. Again the disparities are strong. We jump from an old man to a young man, from outdoors in winter to inside at an indeterminate time of day and year, from a turning figure to one staring straight ahead out of the screen. The jump-cuts continue through a series of seven shots, treating time with great freedom as Cotten demonstrates changing fashions in menswear:

> With evening dress a gentleman wore a tan overcoat, so short that his black coat-tails hung visible five inches below the overcoat. But after a season or two he lengthened his overcoat till it touched his heels and he passed out of his tight trousers into trousers like great bags.

The narrator's interest in developments in fashion stands in contrast with his lack of response to the individuals modelling the hats, shoes, trousers and coats. They remain as nameless as they are voiceless, characterised only through the clues that their looks and gestures offer to the eye. None of them is performing an action that informs us of much beyond leisured prosperity and a general, smiling satisfaction with self and world. Clearly Welles intends to establish his characters first as figures anonymously representative of their times, and only gradually to have them emerge as individuals. For the moment, too, he is holding his actors off from full engagement with their parts. The figure parading before us in trousers like great bags is still Joseph Cotten, posturing and going through his moves. Other members of the cast (notably Agnes Moorehead) appear, in this early part of the film, insecurely identified with the characters they will later present. There is a lot of playfulness in their playing.

On the other hand, vital work is being done with what will become the character of Eugene Morgan. Four of the shots have him studying his image in a mirror, and all of them show him committed to modish trivia. Callow, with a young man's narcissism, this is a figure unlike the mature Eugene. The memory of it might account for the older man's understanding of young folly as he later encounters it in Georgie Minafer. More importantly, by settling on this figure as the one to take us through shoes and trousers and coats, the film is not only confirming him as a main character but also fixing him in our eyes within a mould of repetition. He does everything twice: tries hats, changes shoes, models overcoats. Finally he is doubled even within the one act. The camera is positioned in front of a heavily-framed long mirror, so that as the short

Eugene's doubled entrance

overcoat is tried the figure first enters the mirror image, approaching the camera, and then comes into the frame through the left foreground, back to the camera, as he moves forward for a closer view of the tails. The process is reversed when he goes, so that his image exits first through the foreground and then from the mirror. This doubled effect is itself offered for a second time when he reappears to try the long overcoat. The series ends with a last echo of the mirror entrance when, stepping out into the sunlight to leave his house, the vain fellow walks forward into view through the on-screen frame of the front door.

The succession of shots has, slyly, assembled a picture of a young man's getting dressed to go out, taking him from underwear to outdoor costume. It has also dressed the actor, readying him for the character's definitive moment in this prologue, his rejection by his sweetheart.[19] This will be represented by a much weightier repetition, taking up the motif of

Eugene turned away at the door of the mansion

entrances and exits: Eugene Morgan – he will now acquire the name – calls twice at the Amberson mansion expecting to make up with Isabel and is twice answered at the door and sent from it by the butler Sam. The pattern of this double rebuff was precisely prepared by the costume-change episode – the same use of ellipsis couples two distinct occurrences of approach and retreat. The new feature is diegetic sound; each attempt starts with the ringing of the doorbell and the second ends with Sam saying 'Miss Amberson aint at home to you, Mr Morgan.' The words that forbid Eugene access to the house will have their echo, years later, in 'You're not wanted in this house, Mr Morgan.' The perspective is different for this first dismissal; the view is from outside the house, with Eugene.

The character of Eugene emerges from typicality into a fuller presence by acquiring speech and a voice inflected with emotion. He is the first of the main characters to achieve this solidity, and it is given to

Sending Eugene away ...

... a different perspective

him in the scene of his disappointment. His moment of selfhood in the film comes in his repeated rejection and in his repeated acceptance of rejection.

Isabel's spurning of Eugene is pictured for us, but not the deed that follows from it, her marriage to Wilbur Minafer. At this point Eugene disappears from view, but Wilbur hardly ever comes into it. Eugene's place at the centre of the story is taken instead by Isabel's child Georgie. The account of the next nineteen years is organised round incidents in George's growth to young manhood. We hear nothing of Eugene and see next to nothing of the Minafers' marriage. Strikingly Isabel's acquisition of speech comes late and it comes in a scene which gives her, though her husband is present, fully the role of a mother – gently reproving but also defending the little miscreant who is her son and the love of her life.

At the cusp of these developments, when Eugene was setting out with gifts to placate Isabel, voice was granted to the townspeople and fragments of their conversation were immediately allocated some of the commentary functions of the narrator. Anonymous townsfolk were constituted as a chorus to expand on Ambersonian splendour, concentrating in the first place on its display in the extravagance of the Amberson mansion which is seen, with them, from the outside. ('Sixty thousand dollars for the woodwork alone!') The development of this device embeds in the textures of the film the various tonalities of gossip along with the sense of Amberson doings, public and private, as the focus of this small community's interest. It also puts in place the final element necessary for the elaboration of the montage patterns that govern this sector of the movie.

Townsfolk as chorus (male)

Townsfolk as chorus (female)

The film's game with time has become boisterous and unpredict-able. We are invited to share in pleasure at the plasticity of image and sound, their openness to interruption, displacement and manipulation. A single exclamation follows the statement of the woodwork's cost: 'Hot and cold running water upstairs and down, and stationary washstands in every last bedroom in the place!' But these words are split between three voices of contrasted character (and gender) and across two images of quite distinct shape and content. There is continuity in the world represented but not in the means or the density of representation. Some episodes are fully realised although uprooted, their characters active in identifiable social settings – the barber's, the dressmaker's. At other points the speakers are speakers only, isolated from their own lives and contexts against blank backgrounds of empty sky to deliver their views of Amberson actions and prospects.

Welles can now interweave commentary with remarks, some extended, some fragmentary, from figures within the film's world, and he can use these remarks either with or without the on-screen presence of the speaker so that the sound montage sometimes runs with and sometimes departs from the process of the image. As with that first 'Yoohoo!' the voices of the story world have no sooner found their place in the film's soundstream than they enter into dispute with it, challenging its tone and its rhythms first and quite soon its data.

So the story of the Minafer marriage and its most significant outcome is first entrusted, before the event, to the imposing Mrs Foster. She sits in her undies at the dressmaker's opining on Isabel's motives and then predicting: 'She'll be a good wife to him, but they'll have the worst

The prophetess: 'The worst
spoiled lot of children ...'
Mrs Foster at the dressmaker's

spoiled lot of children this town will ever see.... She couldn't love Wilbur, could she? Well, it'll all go to her children, and she'll ruin them.' Frisky music enters on the firm nod with which Mrs Foster seals her certainty and the image dissolves to an apparently unrelated sight, a daytime view down the town's unmetalled highway to the distant junction, with no evident centre of interest. Welles' voice comes in over: 'The prophetess proved to be mistaken in a single detail merely... Wilbur and Isabel did not have children; they had only one.' This does not just correct Mrs Foster; it also puts her statement a good way into the past. But, with the street image held, her voice is heard again: 'Only one! But I'd like to know if he isn't spoiled enough for a whole carload.' This time her comment emerges from no given situation. All we can know, if we bother to think about it, is that this demand is being made years after her recently heard observations, years enough for a baby of Isabel's now to have grown into a boy displaying his spoiled nature. Mrs Foster is no longer giving her views to the sewing circle but appears to be engaging across the decades with the film's narrator. Welles responds and once more puts the woman's voice into the past: 'Again she found none to challenge her. George Amberson Minafer, the major's one grandchild, was a princely terror.'

Meanwhile the image presents a different event, an unmentioned event, on a contrastingly stable time-scale – that of perfect, real-time continuity. The extended, unfilled duration of the shot slows the pace to accommodate the passage of years. The camera remains completely fixed, refusing to adjust to the main development in front of it, as from the far distance a pony and trap drive down the street toward us. By the

The princely terror

time of 'Only one!' the vehicle's progress can be perceived as the image's key action. Its movement continues swift, steady but not of clearly defined interest until it is close to the camera. Just after Welles has mentioned the major's grandchild, and just before it careers out of frame through the left foreground, the trap passes through a shaft of light that flashes us a vision of the ringleted lad holding the reins. These few frames coincide with the words 'princely terror'.

This sample must serve to exemplify the amazing and delightful intricacy of the sequences that whip us through the early life of Georgie Minafer. The different lines of continuity compete, clash, converge and resolve before splitting off again in new patterns. It is like weaving and something like a fugue, the various strands running with and against each other thrillingly. Collisions and interruptions that might kill the rhythm vary it instead, yielding a syncopation that gives energy and surprise to the film's movement. Time and again continuity is recovered from the shifts that seem to break it so as to produce a new and unexpected mesh.

As Georgie Minafer is born into the film in the role of brattish daredevil, playfulness in Herrmann's music both indulges him and underscores the buoyant ingenuity of the presentation. Some of Welles' brilliance in this section is subtle and likely to escape notice, like the invention of the barber shop and the dressmaker's as settings for male and female gossip. This is a choice of locations so immediately identifiable that they need no preparation and no mention. They can give variety of visual character and dramatic tone without slowing the picture's movement with a need for explanations.

The cleverness is also quite often on display, offered for our

Uncle Jack at the barber's
'Wilbur may not be any
Apollo ...'

enjoyment. Movements through time and space that are not absorbed into the and-next-ness of storytelling will necessarily draw attention to constructedness, to artifice and the artificer. The fictional world exists in our minds independent of the medium or the mode of representation. (It makes sense to wonder whether King Lear was an only child but we do not enquire how Carmen came to be trained as a soprano.) Yet the world exists in and on the film as a construct, subjected to the film-maker's selection and manipulation. It is a fact about the fictional world that, soon after his pony ride through town, Georgie told an outraged citizen to go to Hell. It is not, though, an event on the screen since the censoring of the word 'Hell' is made blatant. The more fragmentary and displaced the choice of sounds and images the more overt are the creative acts of picking and placing. As with the elided 'Hell' the film can joke with us about its own selections.

Welles plays the succession of images and sounds in the film so that it is palpably distinct from the succession of events in the fiction. In a presentation apparently master-minded by him as the narrator, he sets the world in argument with his claims. The most extreme instance comes when the voice-over is musing on Georgie's transgressions and on the longing with which the townsfolk anticipated 'his comeuppance'. The words are immediately challenged by an on-screen questioner with 'His what?' Welles carries his disposition of commentary and action close to the absurdity whereby these figures from the past would seem to be hearing what he now has to say about them. Part of the result is a declaration, embedded in the tone, that this is a world in whose recollection and representation we can have fun.

Fondness. Buoyancy. Fun. Ceaselessly paraded invention. But what is it that the film covers in this exhilarating fashion? Clumsiness, rejection and foolish pride; disappointed hopes; loveless marriages, one shown, another passed over in silence; and a child of energy and spirit growing up confused and learning arrogance in the care of a mother who treats him as the only thing of value her marriage has brought her. A system of euphemism is continuously in place. Everything is jokes and pranks. Isabel's rejection of Eugene is shown in humorous mime. The emptiness of her marriage is a prediction amusingly offered, then confirmed only in glancing implication – 'The prophetess was wrong in a single detail merely....'

The key scene is the one that follows little Georgie's deleted expletive. In Welles' shooting script and in the storyboards Isabel's attempt at reproof is a scene between her and Georgie alone, witnessed in silence by the butler. In a late and important change, Sam was replaced by Wilbur Minafer and George's grandfather, Major Amberson. The effect is to offer us a portrait – just this one – of the home life of the Minafers. The scene now starts with Wilbur attempting a rebuke, but his words are mere recitation. Quoting with concern from the citizen's letter of protest he sounds prissy and servile, already defeated: 'This was heard not only by myself but by my wife and the lady who lives next door.' When George cuts in to dismiss his accuser as an old liar, Wilbur's reading is suspended, never to be resumed. He is immediately displaced from the action but held in the image by a fixed camera so that we see him sidelined. The sequence becomes a conversation between mother and son in which Isabel seeks to excuse Georgie while the Major laughs

The home life of the Minafers

infectiously at his grandson's lordliness. Wilbur meanwhile sits ignored and excluded, unprotesting as he hears Georgie refer to himself as an Amberson. The sketch is full of fun, with George engagingly unrepentant, getting the last mischievous word, and the Major as robustly supportive as Isabel is tenderly unable to chide. At the end a playful clarinet takes us out of the scene in merriment. Nothing in the tone with which the episode is offered acknowledges what it plainly shows – that George is not a happy or a fortunate child nor one who is being sensibly prepared for the world.

Rendering events of bitter implication with humour and aplomb, Welles presents through form the possibility of seeing this past as a time of enchantment. He invites us to collude in understanding the world as Amberson-centred and always interesting never drab, exuberant in its power and harmless in its frailties. But he plants within our collusion an awareness of its willed and partial aspect. Welles as director knows what Welles as speaker prefers to forget. The director sets in place challenges to the narrator's authority so that the tone and content of the commentary become elements in – where we would expect them to give definitions of – the film's pattern and significance.

Through shape and style this prologue section of the film embeds what will only gradually emerge in its drama, the conflict of knowledge and sentiment, judgment and feeling, of which as a young man George Minafer will become the focus. In a scene of magical simplicity towards the end of the movie, a scene whose charm owes much to Ray Collins' humbled but resilient and not really chastened demeanour, Uncle Jack at his leaving will tell George 'I've always been fond of you…. I can't say I've always liked you.' He will go on to suggest that Lucy Morgan is 'somebody else in this town who's always felt about you like that, fond of you … no matter how much it seems you ought to be hanged'.

Lucy's experience of finding herself in love with someone that she cannot respect, whose actions and attitudes her judgment rejects, will become a differently resolved counterpart to Isabel Amberson's blind adoration of her son. In another of those scenes that one could willingly exchange for the entire output of many a gifted film-maker, Lucy will explain herself through the fabrication of a legend. That it is so clearly a fabrication is the mark that she cannot quite be sure of the depth or permanence of her conviction. It is the story of Rides-Down-Everything, a bad Indian chief whose tribe sent him into exile: 'They

Uncle Jack's farewell: 'Two gentlemen of elegant appearance in a state of bustitude'

didn't want him back, of course ... but they weren't able to discover any other warrior that they wanted to make chief in his place. They couldn't help feeling that way.'

The pull between intellect and affections seems to me much deeper in the film than the social history chronicle that critics have often proposed as the source of its interest. In the opening section of the film it is communicated through Welles' way with montage. In other hands, like Eisenstein's, montage is an extreme process of bending the world to the will of the creator but Welles uses it to insist on variety of perspective. The intricacy of his cutting, in and between image and sound, issues a playful challenge to the order he constructs so that it works to express the artist's conflict between pride in control and self-distrust. He has found a way to have the world he creates mock the folly of those who would think to offer a settled view of it.

3

. . . .

TRANSITION

With Georgie's growth to young manhood the film's manner changes. A form derived from montage and a continuity largely given in voice-over yields to one based on scenes developed in depth and at length, often without cutting and with an elaborately mobile camera. The change, and the completion of the prologue, is marked by the disappearance of the narrating voice. It will not be heard again until after Isabel's death and the decay of the Amberson fortune. Its remarks here signal the end of exposition and synopsis as they prepare an event of great moment:

> When Mr George Amberson Minafer came home for the holidays in his sophomore year nothing about him encouraged any hope that he had received his comeuppance. Cards were out for a ball in his honour, and this pageant of the tenantry was the last of the great long-remembered dances that everybody talked about.

Since nothing so far has indicated any loss of magnificence a new mood is set by the word 'last' and by Welles' delivery of the phrases that follow it in a heart-catching tone of regret. The words accompany the camera's entry into the Amberson mansion and our first look inside. It is placed to make a big event out of the opening of the double doors as we sweep in from a snow-covered and wind-blown outside following close behind a man and a woman overcoated against the cold. The man will soon turn

Eugene and Lucy arrive at the ball

Isabel greets Eugene at the ball; George observes

out to be Eugene Morgan, now a middle-aged widower. So the ball is the occasion for his entry into the house previously barred to him, as it will be also for his reunion with Isabel, and the meeting of his daughter Lucy with George.

This is the first time that those doors have parted for Eugene. Their opening encourages the hope of a second chance. The opportunity to undo the mistakes of the past is extended across the generations to Eugene's daughter and Isabel's son. The mood is fostered by presenting the luxurious spaces of the mansion as a refuge and by an initial stress on the most elegant and attractive aspects of the Amberson way of life. One of the first things we shall observe is the gorgeousness of Isabel's ball gown. Then the decor is finely flattered in photography which by-passes a distractingly realistic simulation of gaslight in order to provide, in depth and sparkle, lustrous images of confident, profligate, apparently inexhaustible prosperity. Camera movement is elaborately choreographed to weave through many zones of action. Its unhurried fluidity enhances the sumptuousness of the display. Even in RKO's sadly abbreviated form this ball scene proclaims a definitive change of pace.

In the movies pace is meaning. The scene captures a beguiling courtliness, benign in its hospitality to rough humour and for the most part affectionate and kindly in its condescensions. We are drawn into a mood that appreciates Lucy Morgan's amused and teasing response to George, whose blinkered arrogance is fully displayed but too foolish to be threatening. This mood wants her, against her better judgment, to fall for him. He is a young idiot but she has sense and spirit enough for two; and she is lovely. Perhaps he can be re-educated, redeemed. She may be *his* second chance.

In this mood high spirits are not brought down by the sombre aspect of Eugene's remarks about second chances. Visibly intoxicated by his reunion with Isabel and the warmth of his welcome into the Amberson circle, Eugene can happily mock Uncle Jack's thought that old times are starting all over again: 'Old times? Not a bit. There aren't any old times. When times are gone, they're not old, they're dead! There aren't any times but new times.' Yet despite the cheerful emphasis with which he bats out the word 'dead' there is ambivalence here. It comes from the tension between the vigour of conviction in Joseph Cotten's speech and the wistfulness of his tones. This actor's voice is always within a soft and yielding register; he is no good at shouting. The voice is most itself in moods of defeat, ruefulness, or sympathy with another's pain. Its Virginian[20] gentility colours any progressive assertion with an attachment to the past, a preference for the world once imagined over the world now known.

What is strongest through the ball scene, though – at least in what we have of it – is an enveloping warmth that comes from a sense of tender regard, fellowship in cherished memory, renewed hope and the charm of friendship – perhaps romance – in the making. These moods are carried over into the famous sequence of the ride through the snow where George's horse and sleigh enter into contest with Eugene's automobile and which ends with everybody singing 'The Man Who Broke the Bank at Monte Carlo'. The winter scene is shaped to give it the aspect of a golden world. The cold is convincingly rendered, but with a special shading: this is not a cold that bites in to you, but one that makes you appreciate the comfort of your furs. No chill wind blows. In the pretty bleakness of the snowscape the characters show the nonchalance of folk who are sure of a warm fireplace.[21]

The fame of the scene derives in part from Welles' having filmed it in an icemaking plant, with the attendant expensive difficulties. A fetish for authenticity was clearly not the motive since the setting has throughout a beguiling artificiality. The added element that reaches the screen as a result of filming in an ice-house rather than in the heat of a film studio is the condensation of the actors' and horse's breath on the air. Its vapour creates an image of new-minted purity to contrast with the smoke that befouls the air as it issues from the exhaust of Eugene's horseless carriage.[22] The negative side of this contrast belongs to the motor car, whose ultimate triumph is known to us. The characters, in

George and Lucy at the ball: 'The last of the great long-remembered dances'

these moments of happy ignorance, look threatened as their world displays to our eyes so clear a token of its doom.

The note of threat is often heard in this part of the picture, sometimes subduing though most often submerged by the warmer tones. It is strongest in the scene that comes between the ball and the sleigh ride. Here we see the inside of the Amberson mansion in a different aspect and what was previously obscured comes before our eyes. The house built in the exuberance of new, apparently inexhaustible wealth is built for public life, to receive admiring crowds. When not lit for show and animated by a throng its spaces become oppressive, eerily shadowed and with a cavernous echo. A whisper is apt to travel beyond the ears it is meant for. Privacy or intimacy is hard to find.

A farewell dance between Isabel and Eugene makes this clear, with a romantic suggestion of longings that may not be acknowledged and that have to be contained within admissible forms. There is sadness in the knowledge that this 'Toujours ou jamais' is the last waltz in the last of the great long-remembered dances. The departed crowd, the carpets that await resetting over the dance floor, and the musicians retained beyond the needs of hospitality all point to the moment as leaning on the edge of the acceptable. But it takes place as a matter of observation and comment by the couple's children, and it ends to the applause of Uncle Jack.

The echo in spaces not made for domesticity first reaches our ears when Aunt Fanny intervenes from afar with 'You little silly!' upbraiding George for remarks not addressed to her, remarks against Eugene. The argument that follows is set in the corridor approach to Fanny's bedroom, not a space that guards the closeness of their exchange. It carries so well that Uncle Jack's voice is heard in protest from an adjoining room, vowing to move to a hotel. This scene anticipates the transformation of the great staircase from a social space of elegant conviviality where movement flows easy and unhurried. It becomes steep and gaunt with changes of light and use, a site of spying, whispered conspiracy and recrimination, one that is laborious to climb and hazardous to descend.

More than anything else it is the introduction of the character of Fanny Minafer that qualifies the charm and gaiety of these congenial scenes. Fanny comes into the film, at the ball, along with the grown-up George, as an equal product of the Amberson world and as a figure to offset both her sister-in-law Isabel and the other new arrival, Lucy. In Agnes Moorehead's gallant, pain-wracked performance we are presented with a woman who lives with the knowledge that her unhappiness is a joke, that when exposed it makes her a figure of fun, not of sympathy. She seldom unbends, never ceases to calculate her moves, and the tightness in her throat shrills her voice. The fear of the world's mockery forbids direct expression of her most vital thoughts so that she is constrained to a deviousness by which she herself is humbled. At the ball, her first remark[23] poses as a compliment to her brother Wilbur; he 'not only got [Isabel] but kept her'. The concealed purpose of the remark is to remind Eugene that Isabel is a married woman who, when she had the choice, spurned him. A more public motive is to draw Eugene's attention to herself. In this it fails. Without intending a slight, without giving the matter thought of any kind, Eugene turns his back on her to enquire how Lucy is faring, then makes off to take up the Major's offer of a Havana cigar.

To others she is 'Poor old Fanny'. To herself, unguarded, she becomes 'Ridiculous old Fanny'. What makes her so is her manless state and, more particularly, just that thing that gives Isabel charm and allure – her longing for Eugene Morgan. The difference between Fanny and Isabel is played out around the word 'ridiculous'. On the automobile trip through the snow, the vehicle and Isabel are the twin centres of Eugene's concern, Fanny a kindly regarded accessory. Faced with Isabel's fussing over her son, Eugene tells her she is 'the same Isabel I used to know ... a divinely ridiculous woman'. He rejects the interpretation by which these terms cancel out so that Isabel becomes 'nothing in particular', and he insists that the words be taken positively, as an expression of esteem and affection. Still, we can hear that 'the Isabel I used to know' means 'the woman who won my love' and that to be divinely ridiculous is the essential condition for desirability.

In a world that, or for a man who, defines the ideal in this way Fanny is condemned to spinsterhood. Soft, adoring acquiescence is a posture she cannot sustain. When she tries it, it rings false and makes her look silly. After Eugene's words to Isabel the next we hear from Fanny is some chat about his automobile experiments: 'He says he's going to have wheels all made of rubber and blown up with air. I should think they'd explode.' What could be an intelligent lay person's expectation is delivered with a fluttery shrillness. Although the remarks are made to Lucy we see that they are designed to reach Eugene, and to display the speaker in divinely ridiculous mode. Only the ridiculous aspect is achieved. The happy blindness that Isabel enjoys (until it kills her) is not available to Fanny. She is too clear-sighted and too conscious of energy to exist contentedly within the available roles. She cannot repress the sharpness of perception that earlier issued in an acerbic comment on the lifelessness of her beloved brother Wilbur: 'he never wants to go anywhere that I ever heard of.'

Fanny is the character for whom the gulf between public display and concealed feeling is widest and most tormenting. She becomes the prisoner of the Amberson mansion, trapped in the role of Aunt more narrowly than Isabel is self-confined in the role of Mother – aware of being valued mainly for the quality of her cake-making. The animosity that George can never directly express towards his mother gains expression in thoughtless, sanctioned cruelty towards Fanny. But in the ball and snow scenes panic and dread have not entirely displaced hope in Fanny's view of her future; she is shrewd enough to cultivate Lucy's friendship. Eugene's return can look like a second chance for Fanny too. 'It seems so like old times,' she says, 'to hear him talk.'

4

. . . .

FALLING APART

At the close of the snow scene an end that is more than the end of a sequence is marked by the use of a silent movie device. An iris effect shrinks a ring of darkness round the car with its merrily singing riders as, far off, it heads toward the brow of a hill. Emphatic in itself as a declaration of closure, the device also takes full circle the pattern of anachronism set out in the film's opening shots.

It is the death of Wilbur, not the growth to manhood of his son, that brings an end to the golden aura of nostalgic recall. An event through which romance between Isabel and Eugene seems to enter the realm of possibility, it is presented with a heaviness out of proportion to Wilbur's material or emotional significance. The bitter tone of the

Iris out

imagery finds its match in the face of Fanny Minafer, puffed with anguish as she contemplates the corpse of her brother and the death of her hopes. Taking us into the new situation on Fanny's despair rather than on the necessarily ambiguous emotions of Eugene or Isabel, Welles marks a decisive turn in the mood with which the failures and follies of the past are to be regarded.

On the fade-in, the door imagery is restated. The doors are seen close-up from outside, with a black wreath signifying that the Amberson mansion has become a place of mourning. Eugene's shadow falls across the doors. We hear the muffled chimes of the doorbell; they seal the sense of repetition. Sam opens the door and Eugene's shadow enters before he

The death of Wilbur Minafer;
Eugene arrives as a mourner

himself passes through with Lucy. The door then shuts across the camera, the click of its latch given precedence in the sound balance over the death-laden music. There is a strong contrast with the start of the ball scene, where the camera swept into the mansion with Lucy and Eugene. Now Eugene's entry has been filmed as a shutting out. We shall not see him cross this threshold again.

The completion of the pattern occurs in two stages. First George takes the role played at the start by the butler and closes the door on Eugene when he comes calling. ('My mother will have no interest in knowing that you came here.') The repetition is evident; it extends to a preparatory image of George observing Eugene's approach from behind a lace-curtained window upstairs. But there is change as well; this time we see the shutting door from within the mansion. Finally, as Isabel lies dying, Eugene's attempt to visit her is defeated and George again

George observes Eugene's
approach

George watches …

… Eugene's departure

watches his departure from inside and above, taking what was once Isabel's view. This imagery pictures the degree to which George sees himself as acting for his mother, but also his imposition of a regime of desire and denial that eradicates Isabel. It marks the completion of George's development from prankster to law enforcer.

The pattern remains visible, just, through the RKO butchery that is at its most damaging in the scenes concerning George's oppression of Isabel and banishment of Eugene. Up to that point the studio made a mutilated version of Welles' film. At and beyond that point it composed its own clumsy drama out of materials many of which were of Welles' creation.[24]

It becomes inappropriate to discuss *The Magnificent Ambersons* as a coherent work. Instead I shall turn to one striking aspect that does survive coherently and excitingly in the film as we have it: the use of the long take. The film's appeal to cinephiles is partly due to its brilliance and versatility in exploring long-take techniques. Welles' effectiveness with the long take owes something to his tact; it is not a technique bigotedly imposed on the material, but one that takes its place within the director's repertoire as an aspect of his genius in editing, and in relating editing to *mise en scène*.

Some of the 'long takes' are not particularly long but they earn the description because they are sequence shots where continuous action is filmed continuously, without segmentation. In the prologue section of the film, for instance, the scenes at the barber's and dressmaker's, and the attempted reproof to young Georgie,[25] are all shot in this way and take their place as illustrative sketches within the overall pattern of montage. Conversely some sequences are elaborately edited. The snow scene required a wide variety of set-ups so as to contruct the sense of an outdoors excursion within the limits of the ice-plant studio.

More significantly, the sequence of George's first challenge to Eugene is shot from many angles and, at times, quite rapidly cut. That is because the scene takes place with Eugene as a guest in the Amberson dining room, with the six characters seated at both sides and both ends of the dinner table. The formality of the arrangement is essential to the scale of the transgression in George's attack on Eugene's business when he butts in across the older man's reflections with 'Automobiles are a useless nuisance.' With this *mise en scène*, a long take would have involved either a grotesquely nimble camera or too restricted an account of reactions round the table, since very few of the faces could be visible at any one time.

The scene shows some of the advantages of conventional analytic editing, its flexibility, its immediacy of response to dramatic developments, its ability to use the impact of visual shock in the instant transformation of the image, and its capacity for eloquence in playing with and against our interests and expectations. Here, for instance, the aggression in George's rudeness is stressed by having his voice barge across the soundtrack while we are seeing a two-shot with the Major listening to Eugene. Their eyes turn to George, off-screen – a larger movement of Eugene's head than of the Major's. Two quick cuts give us close-ups of Uncle Jack and Isabel, lost for words. Close shots now predominate until Eugene's departure, as if the shock of George's behaviour has broken the group into individuals struggling separately

George (off-screen):
'Automobiles are a useless
nuisance'

with conflicting thoughts and feelings. But close-ups of the principals, George and Eugene, are delayed. The issues of how far George will sustain his attack and how strongly Eugene will respond are left before us while we take in the bewilderment of the others and the embarrassed silence of Isabel. Then, while Uncle Jack's voice from off-screen attempts the reproof that Isabel needed to speak, we arrive at the close shot of Eugene, eyes down as he reaches for a dessert spoon with one hand and his thumb slowly teaches itself the smooth hardness of the silver. This constructs the sense, when Eugene does begin to speak, of his doing so in a considered response and seeking both to speak truthfully and to negotiate the conflicts round the table. It is, as it had to be, one of Joseph Cotten's great moments:

> I'm not sure George is wrong about automobiles…. With all their speed forward they may be a move backward in civilisation…. It may be that they won't add to the beauty of the world or the life of men's souls. I'm not sure. But automobiles have come, and almost all outward things are going to be different….

As he begins Eugene is looking towards George in acknowledgment that his speech is not only a contribution to a discussion of civic issues. The shot is by far the longest held in the sequence; the reduced rate of cutting produces a concentration that dwells on the sense of sober reflection, and gives full weight to the tension between the balanced assessment offered in his words and the tone of regret that inflects his voice. Our familiarity with the fixed positions of the off-screen characters round the table

Eugene considers his words: 'I'm not so sure that George is wrong ...'

means that every movement of Cotten's eyes is meaningful as an address or an avoidance, and we can feel the pull between the inwardness of his concern with the world he is helping to create and his effort to control the effect of his exposition at this moment, in this company. His hand continues to work at the spoon, absorbing his agitation, and displaying it to us. When he has nearly completed his speculations he glances at his antagonist, seeking an accommodation with 'It may be that George is right....' A cut to George looking down to refuse this offer leads to a bigger close-up of Eugene (that excludes his hand) as he continues to speak softly but, after a last glance has found no change in George's obduracy, allows himself a disguised expression of anger by ending – in a tone of acquiescence that denies the mockery – with a repetition of the clumsy form of words in which George attempted to justify his assault: some time in the future, he concedes, he may not be able 'to defend the gasoline engine, but would have to agree with George – that automobiles "had no business to be invented".' Unseen, but registered in sound, his dropping the spoon onto the table announces an end to his efforts.

This sequence is followed closely by the first of the two scenes between George and Aunt Fanny which take place on the staircase. It is filmed in a single take lasting close to three minutes and making use of a stealthy camera that (in a movement of unflaunted virtuosity) tracks their ascent. The relationship between the action of the camera and the movements of the actors is managed so that claustrophobic continuity is built while a dramatically pointed variety is achieved in the image. The actors pass through areas of shadow, and the varying intensity and direction of the light yield a graded distribution of emphasis on their

George and Fanny's first
staircase scene; the ascent

faces and gestures. At the start Fanny waylays George and in congratulating him shows insight into his motives while he – not for the first time – denies having any motive at all. His refusal to examine his own action is aptly pictured in his turning his back on Fanny and attempting to get away from her. Then the laborious exertion of the climb, with its possibilities of evasion and pursuit, gives an effectively strenuous tone to an interaction in which Fanny lets slip the claim that the whole town is gossiping about Eugene and Isabel, and is then torn between satisfaction and panic at George's response. The charged significance of off-screen space remains available for use. At the end of the scene George dashes away to confront a neighbour. The camera stays on Fanny as her eyes follow George's descent, and show in the continuity of their movement the failure of her efforts to call him back.

Here and elsewhere Welles shows a masterful ingenuity in devising

Fanny: 'George! What are you
going to do, George?'

ways to have the actors' faces available to the camera within the long take, while avoiding constraint on performance and fussy or inexpressive shifts of viewpoint. The long take can give difficulty in face-to-face conversations. That is a circumstance in which the logic of the standard *découpage* can be inescapable, as the 'useless nuisance' scene shows. But there can be drawbacks too in the division of the acting space into separated zones and in the requirement to *favour* (as shooting script jargon correctly puts it) one or another of the characters. In several sequences Welles' use of the long take is adapted to the mobility of the action. By staging the scenes with the actors on the move, walking or riding, he gives himself the opportunity to make both figures – it is usually two – simultaneously and equally visible. At the same time their movement imposes a limit on eye-contact that can give weight to particular moments of inspection or of contact sought and contact evaded.

George and Lucy have two scenes of this sort as they travel together down the main street of the town. The first, about two and a quarter minutes long, has Lucy sitting beside George as he drives his horse and buggy; George presses her to agree to become engaged and blames her refusal on her submission to Eugene's ideals. The second, lasting about three minutes, comes after Isabel has given in to her son's demand that she cut off all contact with Eugene. Lucy seems not to have heard about this when George meets her, by chance, on a walk through town. The camera tracks them as they stroll along the boardwalk. The off-screen world of the growing and changing town is not only audible but visible as well in the reflections caught in the windows of the shops they pass. (A formidable feat of co-ordination.) This second passage is related to the first. On foot, Lucy has an independence from George which is different from her status as his passenger. We may sense from this, and from the frivolously brisk manner in which Lucy responds to his every effort to boost the importance of their relationship, that she has herself in training to cure herself of love for a man that she cannot respect.

Yet her unthought impulse is betrayed (to any eyes more alert than George's) by the ease with which she falls into walking with him, sharing his pace and very soon leaning in to his shoulder in a harmony of movement at odds with her spoken attitudes. This boardwalk scene is a fine example of the subtlety that can be attained when the camera is held back from any display of psychological awareness and discrimination. We are given no prompting to observe motives and responses that the characters withhold. For instance, towards the end of the scene, when George has failed to draw from Lucy any indication of sadness at the news of his imminent departure on a trip around the world, the two of them arrive at a crossroads. In Tarkington the point is insisted upon,[26] so that we are hardly free to ignore its symbolism. But film can be more tactful because it does not need words to make its pictures. The moment is marked, but not remarked, simply by a change in the direction and brightness of the light, when sunshine falls onto the couple from off-screen left as George stops and turns to face Lucy in order to impress her with the finality of their parting.

A vital aspect of Welles' long-take practice is its refusal of the easy rhetoric of emotional and psychological exposure that analytical editing makes available. In conventional practice the timing of the cuts and especially the deployment of close-up provide a means to assert the special significance of a gesture, a glance, a reaction. With the gifted directors the assertion is justified and the image rewards the attention it claims. But the discriminating camera can also sentimentalise perception by applying the rhetoric of insight falsely. It is routine to bang in the close-ups where the drama has no valid climax and where the actor has nothing of substance on display. Welles seems to wish to dissociate himself from the notion that the camera can supply insight not achieved in performance; and his practice can be taken to reflect a recoil from an excessively easy confidence in the camera's assertion of motive and undeclared feeling.

Welles offered a remark full of suggestion when he discussed *Othello* with Bogdanovich.[27] Speaking of the role of Iago he said, 'I think it's a great mistake to try to motivate it beyond what is inherent in the action.' Considered alongside his directorial practice the remark seems to wish to limit the actors' display of the characters' drives and appetites. The likely ground for this is that the projection of the characters' motivations is liable either to place the actors in superiority to their roles or to carry the sense of the characters' awareness of the (now no longer) hidden sources of action, bestowing a rarely appropriate sense of self-understanding.

In such a scene as the boardwalk stroll Welles places great, and thankfully justified, confidence in his actors (as well as in the technicians).

Lucy and George on the boardwalk

Anne Baxter and Tim Holt had to find the means to pace their walk so that after well over a minute they would hit their marks on the street corner at a precise moment in their dialogue; and they had to achieve that without letting George and Lucy appear distracted. At the same time through an extended, oblique exchange they are challenged to keep their action convincing and interesting even when it is not immediately or fully comprehensible. It is not through the promptings of the camera that we may pick up what George is too self-absorbed to notice and Lucy too controlled to display: when George demands some mark of grief from her at the knowledge of his imminent departure, it is not occurring to him that the unexplained fact of the decision and the manner of its announcement may cause Lucy to wonder about the depth of *his* investment in their romance. Immersed in self-justification and self-pity George cannot hear anything beyond the cheery indifference in her tone when Lucy responds with 'If I were you I don't think I'd go' to his complaint that he does not expect to enjoy the trip.

Anne Baxter's performance is very fine, incisive, beguiling. Tim Holt's is quite extraordinary, here and throughout. He is completely free from the actor's vanity that flashes us moments of exaggeration to declare knowledge of the character's defects, to make sure that we go on admiring *him* while we observe the blinkered clumsiness of George Minafer. The performance is funny, as well as appalling, because the actor never steps outside the character's humourless conviction of rectitude and superiority. (Sadly, I suppose this is what the hostiles in the preview audiences detested.) No moment of inappropriate charisma is applied to cover his stiffness, his self-obsession and his bullying. And he never seeks pathos. When the famous strawberry shortcake scene ends with Aunt Fanny in tears, he complains that 'It's getting so you can't joke with her about anything.' Holt gives the line a tone of grievance. George's complaint is that he is being deprived of a source of entertainment. Fanny's breakdown has provoked no insight into her distress and it has not prompted him to consider the cruelty of his teasing.

We may see that George is never free from confusion and a kind of despair. We may think that we have seen their source in his childhood: if Isabel's marriage to his father was a mistake, his own birth is called into question, his place in the world unsecured. But neither elegance nor energy from the actor is allowed to solicit our regard. George never takes on the glamour of a villain. The lack of force is essential to a key element in the tale, that George's command comes from no special power of his own but is created by the weakness of Eugene and Isabel. When he writes to the mother to ask her to stand up against her son, Eugene pleads 'such a little, short strength it would need'. He is evidently right, but 'would need' expects defeat and he nonetheless leaves the task to Isabel.

Very few actors could have given a performance as unselfish as Tim Holt's, and very few directors would have asked for it. Holt's refusal to tip us the wink on his own judgment of George is matched by a camera that does not tip winks of this kind. Though the visual style is as overt as Lang's or Sternberg's or Hitchcock's, and while the cutting can punctuate with pronounced rhythms normal in Hollywood only in farce, these devices are not used to construct a knowledge of character more certain or clear-cut than the knowledge we can derive from deeds and gestures. In my view it is Welles' withholding of camera-constructed guides to the characters' interior lives that underlies André Bazin's wrong-but-right and much debated characterisation of Welles' style in terms of ambiguity and realism.[28]

Sadly for the film, but usefully for the demonstration, one of RKO's bits of vandalism afflicts the boardwalk sequence. In its very last section, after George has left, the long take is punctured by a studio insert: a soft-focus close-up of a tearful Lucy. This comes to interrupt her contemplation of George's departure and to tell us how she *really* feels, by defining her private thought as against her public display. So her composure was mainly for George's deception, and served no significant need of her own. The insert could pose as a clarification. Then we can see that to clarify inappropriately is to change and diminish by giving us just

The RKO insert defines Lucy's true feeling

that simple definition of Lucy's mental state that would – if we took it seriously – make her situation banal and her previous action merely stubborn. The cut into close-up carries the sense of a special truth isolated by the camera's knowing eye. Here it asks too much of the apparatus and almost nothing of the actress. It clarifies by a sudden reduction of our space for thought and wonder.

The complaint is not that the studio's camera discriminates where Welles achieved some kind of neutrality. It is a central fact about photography and so about cinema that the image always displays its viewpoint at the same moment as it displays its subject. The boardwalk scene itself was offering a fine acknowledgment of the camera's need to select before RKO blundered in. George and Lucy are seen in mid-shot, standing at the street corner, when George removes his hat to say a downcast goodbye. The camera pulls back with him, holding Lucy in

Lucy wishes George a splendid trip

frame, as he walks slowly forward. We can see both faces until the moment when George hesitates and turns back towards Lucy to find her still smiling as he says 'I think it's goodbye for good, Lucy.' He turns again and is seen in profile when Lucy offers good wishes for a splendid trip. But then the camera stays put as he claps his hat back on and strides away to the left, so that he leaves the frame to Lucy, still in place in the middle distance. By choosing not to follow George when a choice had to be made the treatment suggests that whereas we have seen all that this incident can reveal about him, there is more to be told about Lucy's part in it. Welles' treatment had its own rhetoric but it was one that expanded, where the studio preferred to narrow, the room in which our understanding could work.

We see this again in another long-take sequence, a little over two minutes long, that stands in absolute contrast with the intricately mobile scenes such as those at the ball or the ones just discussed. When Uncle Jack reports to Eugene and Lucy on what he has seen during a visit to Isabel and George in Paris, the camera stays rigidly fixed in its concentration on three similarly immobile figures. The setting is a grand reception room in Eugene's mansion, lit by electricity and with a fire burning in the chimney place in the far background. Jack is centred in the middle distance, sitting on a divan to the right of a low table. At right angles to him, away from the table, Eugene sits in a wing chair with his legs crossed and his hands folded in his lap – a posture that he holds throughout. Eugene's figure, at the left of the picture, is the most distant but his face is fully lit and most plainly presented to the camera. Facing him, in the right foreground, at the near end of the divan Lucy is attentive but she neither moves nor speaks. With her head turned from the camera she is a vital witnessing presence that makes a difference to the ways in which Jack and Eugene can speak. If she were to intervene by so much as an intake of breath the fact of it would be registered in the men's reactions; but our access to her expression is limited.

We enter the scene, on a dissolve, at a pause in after-dinner conversation. Jack drains his coffee cup and replaces it on the tray with a care that excuses his glancing only briefly at Eugene then Lucy as he starts to speak, weighing his words: 'I found Isabel as well as usual. Only I'm afraid as usual isn't particularly well.' Two things are immediately apparent. The first is that the matter of Isabel has been avoided until the avoidance itself became too burdensome. The second is the delicacy of Jack's position, negotiating between the different responses – in each case predictably complex and guarded – of father and daughter. Each of Ray Collins' movements is eloquent because when he avoids eye contact he looks straight ahead, in profile; if he addresses Eugene his head turns away; his glances at Lucy create the moments when his face is most revealed to us. Since he looks at Lucy very little, avoidance is again given weight. As soon as Jack puts down the coffee cup he reaches for a cigar and through the rest of the exchange he works it between his fingers as a relief from the pressure of Eugene's gaze. The cigar gives him a reason to stay hunched forward, not to lean back into a posture that would promote contact.

Under Eugene's quiet prodding Jack gives his view that Isabel would wish to return home if George would let her. The talk is stilled on the contemplation of George's hold over his mother and some points of unspoken agreement are exchanged through looks and tone on Jack's words '… knowing my interesting nephew as you do … wouldn't you think that ["let her"] was about the way to put it?' (The 'you' excludes Lucy, in kindness.) At this he looks steadily, collusively at his friend, and Eugene replies with – for the first time – a statement rather than a question: 'Knowing him as I do, yes.'

The scene is holdingly, heart-breakingly quiet, visually as well as on the ear. The care put in to the exercise of tact lets us see how embarrassed is the avoidance of embarrassment, but also how delicate is the mutual concern of these friends. Most of all the rigid frame gives an image of the paralysis in which events are held. Submission to George, to Isabel's submission to George, has created a deadlock that only death will break.

Even with so rooted a camera as Welles employs here there is no

Long take, fixed camera:
Eugene, Uncle Frank, Lucy

case for condemning the long take as theatrical. The long take (in fact the duration of any shot) gains its effect in part from the continuous availability of the cut, just as the static camera works as, in part, a refusal of mobility. This must be particularly apparent in a movie that offers extreme alternations between sustained continuity and vigorously disruptive cutting.

The mutually informing relationship between editing and the long take can be seen at work as our sequence starts and ends. We enter on a silence into which, not prompted by any enquiry, Jack inserts his news of Isabel. The ellipse that finds Jack finishing his coffee, and that passes over for instance the initial moments of his reunion with Eugene, is eloquent that only now and at last are the subjects of most significance being broached, and that no way has been found of speaking about Isabel to Eugene without talking to Lucy about George. The lack of movement at the fade-out[29] on Eugene's words of assent uses the rhetoric of an ending to climax the sense of blockage; the meeting between the three is not over, but everything has been said and nothing is to be done.

Throughout the sequence his withholding of reaction shots, most blatantly of the reverse shot on Lucy, shows Welles exploiting the disadvantage of the long take that he finds so many ways of working round elsewhere in the picture: its lack of flexibility in the presentation of face-to-face encounters. A vital consequence of fixity is that all change within the sequence, and all movement except the counterpointing animation of the flames in the background, arises from the actions and gestures of the characters. Far from being a response to some putative unknowability of other minds Welles' refusal of a psychologising camera seems a gesture of confidence in the expressiveness of action and inaction and in the vitally informative function of gestures, hesitations, glances, inflections and so forth – the entire repertoire of behaviours and states of body that the actor can recompose into truthful performance.

Doing without the rhythms of editing within scenes requires the shape and pulse of the action to be found in performance. In long-take technique, as used here, the characters' experience of change, of simultaneity and succession, convergence and separation, anticipation, process and consequence is made more dependent on the being and doing of the actors. The end product is nonetheless a work of art and artifice. The hazards of the extended take increase the probability that dialogue will have to be post-synchronised. On a mobile shot the actors are likely to be specially aware of the always present apparatus because of the constant shunting of items of decor into the camera's view or out of its path. But those are demands on technique and concentration, pre-conditions for performance.

It is importantly the case in the sequences I have discussed that the timing of action and response belongs to the actors. In edited sequences quite a lot of the interaction is constructed at the cutting bench, maybe or maybe not in mimicry of the interactions laid down in a master shot; it is easy to hasten or retard movements, to extend or shorten pauses, to build or subdue reactions, so that the relationships projected on the film are those put together in the editing room and may never have been observed by the apparatus. Welles' method is demanding, but also respectful, of the actors' powers.

Major Amberson: 'the profoundest thinking of his life ...'

5

. . . .

LOSS

The long take opts for one extreme form of the equation between the passage of the spectators' time in the cinema, of the characters' time in the narrative and of the actors' time in performance. In *The Magnificent Ambersons* a particularly forceful juxtaposition of time-scales is involved in embedding stretches of 'real time' in a movie that covers more than twenty years in less than two hours, and that has from the start declared time to be one of its subjects.

One of the strangest and most moving collisions of time comes in the scene that reintroduces the narrating voice, and thereby reinstates the sense of retrospect on a vanished world. 'And now,' we hear, 'Major Amberson was engaged in the profoundest thinking of his life … and he realised that everything which had worried him or delighted him during this lifetime between then and today … was all trifling and waste beside what concerned him now.' The speech is soft, as if fearing to intrude upon an old man of spirit now in his decrepitude. For quite a while[30] we observe the Major's face in a silent flicker of firelight while the narrating voice is heard. The camera is close, getting closer. Then Jack's voice from off-screen prods his memory uselessly with questions about the Amberson estate. The Major's eyes stare out at us, blankly wakeful but still catching the light, as finally he begins to worry aloud at his puzzlement over the sources of life and energy. Nobody could forget the frail, effortful sound of Richard Bennett grappling with the mystery: 'It must be in the sun.…'

The image is in many respects quite abstract; setting and time of day are roughly sketched – somewhere indoors near a fireplace, sometime after dark when others are still active. The presence of the fire is indicated only in an effect of lighting. On the other hand we can see that the Major is sitting there without occupation and he may have been doing so since before dark, as no one has put on the room lights. His concern with heat – the fire, the sun – is the concern of an old man heavily scarf-wrapped, feeling the cold.

One thing we are aware of, even if we do not take note of it: his breathing. Is that Major Amberson's or Richard Bennett's? Both of course. In this at least life and performance are fused. The camera's hanging on the moments of the character's life is necessarily taking moments from the actor's. That is so in a two-second shot as well. But the long take derives effect from its more palpably absorbing some of the reality of the actor's time in its rhythms and pulses. It can become a means of working into the film and making one of its speaking dimensions, the submission to time that is so marked a feature of the photographic subject.

A consequence of the voice-over is to bring into the film understandings of time that belong to spoken language, the ones expressed through the pressure always to give tense to the verbs. The clarity of temporal definition offered by the use of the past tense in the commentary is in a difficult relation to the peculiar relays of time that are involved in our watching an assembly of recorded sound and image. Welles registers, or agitates, the difficulty by introducing his account with *And now* and repeating, concentrating, the references to what we *are* seeing ('now ... today ... now') alongside the reminders of pastness in the verbs: 'was engaged ... had worried him ... what concerned him.' This as the articulation of an image – it tells us what we can *not* see – of a man for whom, as both character and actor, time is running out. The camera's steady gaze, in the film's most sustained close-up, is on a face under erosion by age.

The long take, with its presentation of time-flights that are not only fictional, does seem to draw film-makers who have a particular engagement with time, pastness and loss. Welles, Mizoguchi, Max Ophuls and at key moments Jean Renoir are notable for the way that the steadiness of the camera's attachment to a passage seems gauged to capture movements into the distance, the dying of the light, the fading of an echo, in relation to the longing to hold the moment and to escape with it outside time. *The Magnificent Ambersons* is one of a group of great films that have built the pathos of the photographic into their textures and made it part of their thematic material.

A particular achievement of Welles' film is to have found a form that dramatises the awareness that an attachment to a past, and the piercing sense of its loss, is not dependent on a judgment that it was better than the present, or that its values were ones we should wish to recover. The director spoke about this to Bogdanovich, when the discussion was on his Falstaff movie, *Chimes at Midnight* (1966):

Even if the good old days never existed, the fact that we can *conceive* of such a world is ... an affirmation of the human spirit. That the imagination of man is capable of creating the myth of a more open, more generous time is not a sign of our folly. Every country has its 'Merrie England,' a season of innocence, a dew-bright morning of the world, ... I'm interested really in the myth of the past, *as a* myth.[31]

Tarkington was genuinely a nostalgist, an acute and affecting one for much of the time. Welles can share the sense of the ugliness of the industrial city, and the tone of lament for what it erased, while nonetheless presenting the world of the Ambersons as blinkered in its privilege and subtly self-victimising. Eugene is an enchanting figure of courtliness but predisposed from the start to defeat and regret. Where Tarkington introduced him as 'the person who stepped through the bass viol and had to be assisted to a waiting carriage',[32] Welles completed our first view of the character with him still floored and apologetic. In the development the 'divine ridiculousness' that Eugene admired in Isabel becomes the 'selfless and perfect motherhood' that dooms his second chance.

It was an artistic catastrophe that RKO robbed us of the proper culmination of this theme, an extraordinary moment designed in Welles' script and carried through to the completed film but then eliminated (and replaced by material directed by Robert Wise) in the mayhem inflicted on the scenes of Isabel's capitulation to her son. In Welles' film Isabel wrote a letter to George conveying her submission to his demands. We saw George lying on his bed to read it, then turning onto his stomach so that his back was to the approaching camera, while we heard the text spoken in Isabel's voice. It ended with these lines: 'We'll talk of what's best to do, shan't we? And for all this pain you'll forgive your loving and devoted....' At the very last Welles cut to a close-up of George's face as, in a whisper, he spoke the one final word ' ... Mother'.

We can only imagine this moment, and we may imagine it wrongly. We can derive something of the tone from Bernard Herrmann's score.[33] Soft, slow and thinly orchestrated, it suggests emotions of love and resignation that reflect Isabel's state. There is no note of satisfaction, none of the weight or briskness that might take us into George's response. On the other hand this music was played over the image of

George; it must to some degree have coloured our understanding of his mood. The scene ended here, with George gazing to the foreground and frowning, before the dissolve which took us to the boardwalk scene with Lucy. So the word 'Mother' and George's contemplation of it surely constituted the climax as well as the conclusion of this episode. Welles made two significant changes to Tarkington. He introduced a uniquely cinematic effect, an effect of performance not available to the printed page, through the emphatic break between voices that shattered the conjunction between the time of writing (Isabel's voice) and the time of reading (George's image) that had governed the continuity to this point. He also changed the letter's signature so that the word that George spoke was not the sender's name ('Isabel') but the identification of her role ('Mother').

It seems certain that the intention and the effect must have been to give formal expression to Isabel's confinement within a definition of her role imposed by her son in a way that annihilates her, but a definition of which she herself was the source. The fusion and displacement on the word 'Mother' seem to speak of collusion as well as oppression. The golden, lamented world has yielded a bitter waste of life from both Fanny's strength and Isabel's weakness. RKO's changes can be understood as aimed to redistribute strength and weakness between the characters so as to offer a less uncomfortable view. The withdrawal from 'unpleasant excitement' that Lucy articulates to Eugene in the scene of her Rides-Down-Everything fable, tinged with ambivalence as it is, may well have found its place as a shapely development of the film's concerns, in the Welles version, rather than offering as now an oasis of mutuality and charm amid the scenes of George's comeuppance.

That garden scene offers one of the most touching pictures of the love between daughter and father to be found outside the work of Ozu. It stands as an image of tender acceptance to offset the oppressive outcomes of the love between Isabel and her son. Perhaps in its original context, late in the film, it also presented Lucy in a reasoned but unsatisfying response to the constraints of her father's world, resisting the contrasted forms of ridiculousness, including selfless and perfect motherhood, that we should have seen in Fanny and Isabel.

We shall never know. The camera offers to store the moment and to fix it against time, but sets it down on a material subject to a range of assaults and deformations. The fiction film owes its existence to the

Lucy's fable: 'They couldn't help feeling that way'

aptitude of the moving picture for abstraction from its real context and its arrangement in a new, storymaking sequence. But the same availability to selection and rearrangement that enables the work of the film artist also threatens its survival. So easy to cut. So easy to splice. So easy to throw away.

A movie about loss. A movie that works on, thinks about, film's production of an image haunted by the places and beings from which it derives. But also, in a cruel and arbitrary rhyme, a lost film. So we shall never know what I long to know. That boarding house ending; was it the fine, sad culmination that the story needed, or a wilfully grim denial of hope? Was it a product of Welles the showman, movie-teller, master of mood and discord? Or did it come from that other Welles, the boy wonder hired to redeem Hollywood from the corruption of the popular and the accessible? *That* Welles was available to be drawn into the arid spite and the commitment to misery that blight the Xanadu scenes of *Citizen Kane*. That Welles was boosted by so many for whom 'movie' was a word of contempt and who could see in Hollywood's preferred forms of ending only a traffic in falsity. (Robert Carringer describes the travesty that RKO staged at the end of *Ambersons* as Hollywood's 'typical conception'.)[34]

In plot terms any point of conclusion is arbitrary, chosen. We can go out on a death or a birth. If we end, as so often, on a prospect of marriage we cannot leave with a guarantee of bliss, but we may be encouraged or forbidden to hope. The world does not end with the story's finish. It has a future and the future cannot be closed. So the key question remains at the completion of a movie story as it was throughout, that of the relation between event and viewpoint.

On paper Welles' ending looks inspired. But everything would turn on the question of tone, the balance between pain and compassion, humour and harshness, bleakness and generosity. It might – though none of the witnesses suggests this – have embraced the complacent despair that so often wins acceptance as the authentication of seriousness and Art. We cannot know, because each of us would need to make our own assessment not on the basis of a description but from the experience of the thing itself.

Nothing forbids us to believe Welles when he says of his final scene 'it was pretty rough going for an audience – particularly in those days. But without question it was much the best scene in the movie.'[35] If there is exaggeration here, it is to be found in the comparative aspect. I do not understand that there could be a scene better than so many that the film contains in the only version we can see. *The Magnificent Ambersons* is a film packed with wonders. It has as many marvellous shots, scenes, ideas, performances as most film-makers could hope to achieve in an entire career. So many that in a book-length study I have not found space to treat some of its most famous and stirring delights: the ball scenes, the strawberry shortcake sequence, the ride through town. I have had to omit favourite vignettes, like the one in the lawyer's office where Erskine Sandford enthuses over his profession as 'a jealous mistress and a stern mistress'. And what about the one that ends when Mrs Johnson (Dorothy Vaughn) ejects George into the street with her stiffly piped 'Please to leave my house'? I have not sung, as any study should sing, the achievements of Agnes Moorehead, Ray Collins and Dolores Costello.

A critical study, like a film, chooses where and how to end. I choose to finish with some further thoughts about film and the past. I do not observe this much in women, but among men it is striking how regularly cinephilia is accompanied (as it is in me) by an attachment to the media of sound recording. Many (most?) cinemanes are also big record collectors and lots of them are (like me) promiscuous in the equality of their hunger for discs of, say, Galli-Curci the diva, Arrau the pianist and the singing Mills Brothers or Nellie Lutcher of the fine brown frame. My guess is that this fascination has a lot to do with what André Bazin saw as an embalming impulse underlying film-making. Recording fixes sights and sounds, and segments of living time, making them available for storage so that they can be brought out and replayed at will. Correctly played the media reanimate the performance, in the ideal case without change. The characteristics of both the performance and the recording are recovered at each projection, but the knowledge of repeatability is possibly more significant than any particular experience of repetition.

So film appeals to the collector's appetite, offering comfort in face of time perceived as a destructive force. The past is the past, but we can have it back in this form, to this extent. For a person of such a temperament, disposing of a record is a crisis moment, by all means to be avoided or postponed. Accumulation has its inconveniences but they are more tolerable than loss. Let us suppose then – it seems reasonable – that a film plant must employ many persons of a preserving bent, people spontaneously impelled to take care of threatened celluloid. Why should we rather despair than hope that such a person may have been in place to frustrate the order for the destruction of Welles' film? On top of a cupboard, at the back of an attic, inside a chest, somewhere with an atmosphere convenient to the survival of the film stock, seven reels are stacked, awaiting discovery, a humble studio hand's gift to posterity. That is a good happy ending. It is not a delusion, but it is better than reality.

·

NOTES

· ·

1 Letter (21 March 1942) published in Robert L. Carringer, *The Magnificent Ambersons: A Reconstruction* (Oxford: University of California Press, 1993), pp. 282–3.

2 Main sources on RKO, apart from Carringer and the Welles biographies listed below, are: Richard B. Jewell, *A History of RKO Radio Pictures Incorporated, 1928–1942*, Ph D Thesis, University of Southern California, 1978; Richard B. Jewell with Vernon Harbin, *The RKO Story* (London: Octopus Books, 1982).

3 Booth Tarkington, *The Magnificent Ambersons* (Bloomington: Indiana University Press, 1989), p. 54.

4 Included on the Criterion Collection videodisc edition of the film, CC1109L(1986) from The Voyager Company. A valuable supplementary section produced by Robert Carringer also gives access to the original shooting script, the Campbell Playhouse broadcast, and excerpts from *Pampered Youth*.

5 For instance, from Broadway the Pulitzer prize-winners Robert E. Sherwood's *Abe Lincoln in Illinois* (1940, directed by John Cromwell, loss $745,000) and Sidney Howard's *They Knew What They Wanted* (1940, directed by Garson Kanin, loss $291,000).

6 Carringer, *A Reconstruction*, pp. 261–71.

7 Peter Bogdanovich and Orson Welles, *This is Orson Welles*, ed. by Jonathan Rosenbaum (New York: Harper Collins, 1992). The quote that follows is my rearrangement of material from p. 130.

8 Quoted in Rosenbaum (ed.), *This is Orson Welles*, p. 116.

9 See Note 1.

10 In Carringer, *A Reconstruction*, pp. 286–8.

11 Telegram to Welles from Jack Moss, quoted in Rosenbaum (ed.), *This is Orson Welles*, p. 150.

12 Ibid., p. 122.

13 See Note 1.

14 Rosenbaum (ed.), *This is Orson Welles*, p. 150.

15 Ibid.

16 Jonathan Rosenbaum, 'Pages from the Endfield File', *Film Comment*, Nov–Dec 1993, p. 51.

17 Barbara Leaming, *Orson Welles* (London: Pheonix, 1993), p. 240.

18 Ernest Hemingway, *The Killers*.

19 This is true of both versions, but better organised in Welles' cut. By dubbing between two video recorders it is not difficult to produce an approximation of Welles' ordering of the material.

20 For me as an Englishman one of the most appealing aspects of old Hollywood was the indifference to regional accent that here allowed Cotten to speak in his own voice while playing a character born and reared in Indiana.

21 Thanks to R. W. Emerson and Stanley Cavell.

22 Designed also, in a section cut by RKO, to contrast with the pall of smoke hanging over the town, which is discussed as a consequence of its growth and increasing pollution.

23 In the RKO version, since her first meeting with Lucy has been cut.

24 Rosenbaum (ed.), *This is Orson Welles*, pp. 454–90, offers a clear account of 'The Original *Ambersons*', with dialogue from the cut sequences. As a summary it is less full, but easier reading than the complete cutting continuity script presented in Carringer, *A Reconstruction*.

25 About five seconds, fifty seconds and fifty seconds respectively.

26 Tarkington, *The Magnificent Ambersons*, pp. 378–80.

27 Rosenbaum (ed.), *This is Orson Welles*, p. 233.

28 André Bazin, *Orson Welles, a Critical View*, trans. Jonathan Rosenbaum (London: Elm Tree Books, 1978).

29 A few seconds earlier in RKO's cut than in Welles'.

30 The take was about twice as long in Welles' version as in RKO's.

31 Rosenbaum (ed.), *This is Orson Welles*, pp. 100–1.

32 Tarkington, *The Magnificent Ambersons*, p. 23.

33 Available on disc as Volume One of *The Bernard Herrmann Anthology* from Preamble, PRCD 1783 (1990).

34 In his commentary on the Criterion Collection videodisc edition of the film.

35 Rosenbaum (ed.), *This is Orson Welles*, p. 130.

CREDITS

. . . .

The Magnificent Ambersons

USA
1942
US Release
10 July 1942
Distributor
RKO Radio Pictures Inc
British Release
22 February 1943
British Distributor
RKO Radio Pictures Ltd
Copyright Date
1942

©RKO Radio Pictures Inc
Production Companies
RKO Radio Pictures Inc
Mercury Productions Inc
Producer
Orson Welles
Executive Producer
George J. Schaefer
Production Assistant
Richard Wilson
Unit Business Manager
Fred Fleck
Director
Orson Welles
Additional Directors
Fred Fleck, Robert Wise,
Jack Moss
Assistant Director
Fred Fleck
**Additional Assistant
Director**
Harry Mancke
Screenplay
Orson Welles
Based on the novel by Booth
Tarkington

Director of Photography
Stanley Cortez
Additional Photographers
Russell Metty, Nicholas
Musuraca, Jack McKenzie,
Russell A. Cully,
Harry J. Wild
Camera Operator
Jimmy Daly
Assistant Camera
Howard Schwartz
Gaffer
Jimmy Almond
Process Photography
Clifford Stine
Stills
Alexander Kahle
Special Effects
Vernon L. Walker
Editor
Robert Wise
Additional Editors
Mark Robson, Jack Moss
Design of Sets
Mark-Lee Kirk
Art Director
Albert S. D'Agostino
Set Decorator
Al Fields
Properties
Charles Sayers
Ladies' Wardrobe Design
Edward Stevenson
Make-up
Mel Berns
Music
Bernard Herrmann
Additional Music
Roy Webb
Song
'The Man Who Broke the
Bank at Monte Carlo' by
Fred Gilbert

Sound Recordists
Bailey Fesler, James G.
Stewart
Sound
Earl Mounce, John Tribby,
Terry Kellum
**Stunt Double for
Anne Baxter**
Helen Thurston
Stunt Double for Tim Holt
Dave Sharpe

Cast
Joseph Cotten
Eugene Morgan
Dolores Costello
Isabel Amberson Minafer
Anne Baxter
Lucy Morgan
Tim Holt
George Amberson Minafer
Agnes Moorehead
Fanny Minafer
Ray Collins
Jack Amberson
Erskine Sanford
Roger Bronson
Richard Bennett
Major Amberson

uncredited
Don Dillaway
Wilbur Minafer
Charles Phipps
Uncle John
Dorothy Vaughan
Elmer Jerome
Sam Rice
spectators at funeral

Olive Ball
Mary
Nina Guilbert
John Elliott
guests
Anne O'Neal
Mrs Foster
Georgia Backus
Kathryn Sheldon
matrons
Henry Roquemore
hardware man
Hilda Plowright
nurse
William Elmer
house servant
Edward Howard
Harry Humphrey
Lew Kelly
Maynard Holmes
citizens

Sada Simmons
wife
Gus Schilling
drug clerk
Bobby Cooper
George as a boy
Drew Roddy
Elijah
Jack Baxley
Reverend Smith
Heenan Elliott
labourer
John Maguire
young man
Lyle Clement
man in barber shop
William Blees
youth at accident
James Westerfield
policeman at accident
Philip Morris
policeman
Jack Santoro
barber
J. Louis Johnson
Sam the butler
Mel Ford
Fred Kinney
Robert Pittard
Charles Johnson
Lillian Nicholson
landlady
Louis Hayward
ballroom extra
Nancy Gates
Joe Whitehead
Del Lawrence
Harry Bailey
Edwin August

Orson Welles
narrator

Black and White
7931 feet
88 minutes

Credits compiled by
Markku Salmi,
BFI Filmographic Unit

The print of *The
Magnificent Ambersons*
in the National Film and
Television Archive was
specially prepared for the
360 Classic Feature Films
project from materials held
in the NFTVA

BIBLIOGRAPHY

· ·

Andrew, Dudley, *Film in the Aura of Art* (Princeton, NJ: Princeton University Press, 1984).

Brady, Frank, *Citizen Welles* (London: Hodder & Stoughton, 1990).

Callow, Simon, *Orson Welles, the Road to Xanadu* (London: Vintage, 1996).

Carringer, Robert L., *The Making of Citizen Kane* (London: John Murray, 1985).

Cavell, Stanley, *The World Viewed, Enlarged Edition* (London: Harvard University Press, 1979).

Cavell, Stanley, *Contesting Tears: The Hollywood Melodrama of the Unknown Woman* (London: University of Chicago Press, 1996).

Lasky, Betty, *RKO: The Biggest Little Major of Them All* (Santa Monica: Roundtable, 1989).

McBride, Joseph, *Orson Welles* (London: Secker & Warburg/BFI, 1972).

Naremore, James, *The Magic World of Orson Welles* (New York: Oxford University Press, 1978).

Wilson, George M., *Narration in Light: Studies in Cinematic Point of View* (Baltimore: The Johns Hopkins University Press, 1986).

Wilson, Richard, 'It's Not *Quite* All True', *Sight and Sound*, Autumn 1970.

Wood, Brett, *Orson Welles. A Bio-Bibliography* (Westport, Conn.: Greenwood Press, 1990).

ALSO PUBLISHED

An Actor's Revenge
Ian Breakwell

L'Âge d'or
Paul Hammond

Annie Hall
Peter Cowie

L'Atalante
Marina Warner

L'avventura
Geoffrey Nowell-Smith

The Big Heat
Colin McArthur

The Big Sleep
David Thomson

The Birds
Camille Paglia

Blackmail
Tom Ryall

Boudu Saved from Drowning
Richard Boston

Bride of Frankenstein
Alberto Manguel

Brief Encounter
Richard Dyer

Das Cabinet des Dr. Caligari
David Robinson

Cat People
Kim Newman

Chinatown
Michael Eaton

Citizen Kane
Laura Mulvey

Double Indemnity
Richard Schickel

Les Enfants du paradis
Jill Forbes

42nd Street
J. Hoberman

The Ghost and Mrs Muir
Frieda Grafe

Greed
Jonathan Rosenbaum

Gun Crazy
Jim Kitses

High Noon
Phillip Drummond

In a Lonely Place
Dana Polan

It's a Gift
Simon Louvish

The Life and Death of Colonel Blimp
A. L. Kennedy

Lolita
Richard Corliss

Meet Me in St. Louis
Gerald Kaufman

Napoléon
Nelly Kaplan

La Nuit américaine
Roger Crittenden

Odd Man Out
Dai Vaughan

Olympia
Taylor Downing

Palm Beach Story
John Pym

Pépé le Moko
Ginette Vincendeau

Performance
Colin MacCabe

Queen Christina
Marcia Landy and Amy Villarejo

Rocco and his Brothers
Sam Rohdie

The Seventh Seal
Melvyn Bragg

Shane
Edward Countryman and Evonne von Heussen-Countryman

Singin' in the Rain
Peter Wollen

Stagecoach
Edward Buscombe

Sunrise – A Song of Two Humans
Lucy Fischer

Things to Come
Christopher Frayling

Went the Day Well?
Penelope Houston

Wild Strawberries
Philip and Kersti French

The Wizard of Oz
Salman Rushdie

If you would like further information about future BFI Film Classics or about other books on film, media and popular culture from BFI Publishing, please write to:

BFI Film Classics
BFI Publishing
21 Stephen Street
London W1P 2LN

BFI FILM

CLASSICS

CITIZEN KANE

. . . .

Laura Mulvey

'*An enthralling account of the movie by one of our best film theorists*'
THE GUARDIAN